63 Tactics for Teaching Diverse Learners

Grades 6–12

To all teachers and those they teach . . .

63 Tactics for Teaching Diverse Learners

Grades 6–12

Bob Algozzine
Pam Campbell
Adam Wang

CORWIN
A SAGE Company

For information:

Corwin
A SAGE Company
2455 Teller Road
Thousand Oaks, California 91320
(800) 233-9936
Fax: (800) 417-2466
www.corwinpress.com

SAGE Ltd.
1 Oliver's Yard
55 City Road
London EC1Y 1SP
United Kingdom

SAGE India Pvt. Ltd.
B 1/I 1 Mohan Cooperative
  Industrial Area
Mathura Road, New Delhi 110 044
India

SAGE Asia-Pacific Pte. Ltd.
33 Pekin Street #02-01
Far East Square
Singapore 048763

Printed in the United States of America.

Library of Congress Cataloging-in-Publication Data

Algozzine, Robert.
63 tactics for teaching diverse learners, grades 6-12/Bob Algozzine, Pam Campbell, Adam Wang.
    p. cm.
Includes bibliographical references and index.
ISBN 978-1-4129-4241-6 (cloth)
ISBN 978-1-4129-4242-3 (pbk.)
    1. Middle school teaching. 2. High school teaching. 3. Effective teaching. I. Campbell, Pam, 1942-
II. Wang, Adam, 1956- III. Title. IV. Title: Sixty-three tactics for teaching diverse learners, grades 6-12.

LB1735.5.A45 2009
373.1102—dc22   2008055934

This book is printed on acid-free paper.

09 10 11 12 13 10 9 8 7 6 5 4 3 2 1

Acquisitions Editor:	David Chao
Editorial Assistant:	Brynn Saito
Production Editor:	Eric Garner
Copy Editor:	Paula L. Fleming
Typesetter:	C&M Digitals (P) Ltd.
Proofreader:	Charlotte Waisner
Indexer:	Kathleen Paparchontis
Cover Designer:	Rose Storey

Contents

Preface

Increasingly, students with disabilities and learning differences are in general education classrooms, and teachers are searching for ways to help them meet high academic standards and achieve success. While many recognize that a teacher's expertise is often the critical determinant in any student's achievement, they also realize that meeting the increasingly diverse needs of students calls for additional information and support. In this regard, teachers need easy and simple access to authentic information about teaching and responding to individual differences effectively.

Effective Teaching

63 Tactics for Teaching Diverse Learners, Grades 6–12 is a collection of evidence-based practices designed to help teachers address the instructional needs present in America's classrooms. The book is organized around four components of effective instruction: planning, managing, delivering, and evaluating (cf. Algozzine & Ysseldyke, 1992; Algozzine, Ysseldyke, & Elliott, 1997). It is based on a fundamental belief: teachers are able to respond to individual differences more effectively when provided with an easily accessible resource of effective teaching tips.

63 Tactics for Teaching Diverse Learners, Grades 6–12 provides all teachers (regardless of level, experience, or area of specialization) with access to effective instructional tactics. In developing this book, we used a peer review process that encouraged flexibility and resulted in a collection of teaching activities that help teachers to meet the needs of students in diverse classroom and school settings. *63 Tactics for Teaching Diverse Learners, Grades 6–12* is based on sound models of instruction, and its structure encourages the identification and use of practices that are effective for students with or without disabilities, as well as practices that are designed especially for students with disabilities at middle and secondary grade levels.

Ecological Validity

Ecological validity refers to the extent to which the underlying constructs of an educational model are grounded in logical, representative, and important conditions within the real world of schools. It is a measure of the value, worth, or projected effectiveness of the model. The ecological validity or usefulness of the activities is grounded in considering five assumptions:

1. All children want to learn.
   Ask any child.

2. All children can learn.
   Ask any parent.

3. All schools can educate diverse groups of students.
   Ask any administrator.

4. All classrooms are places where students with varying instructional needs can learn.
   Ask any teacher.

5. All teachers want to teach well so students will learn and succeed; all they need is time, access to information, and sustained support.
   Ask anybody.

Underlying Model

63 Tactics for Teaching Diverse Learners 6–12 is based on a practical model in which four components (i.e., planning, managing, delivering, and evaluating) serve as the base for a set of organizing principles of effective teaching and instruction (see below). The model is grounded in a large and well-accepted body of research on effective teaching. To bring it to life and address the ever-present concern of administrators and teachers for assistance when students fail to profit from instruction, each component and principle is embodied by a set of strategies that represent plans for action in putting theory into practice (see example).

Strategies are steps that should be taken to implement principles and components of effective instruction; they are the "what" of teaching. Tactics are the "how" of teaching—the actions that a teacher can take to influence learning. Tactics are the lowest level a component can be broken into for instructional purposes; they are specific behaviors or teaching activities (see organizational relations).

Components and Principles of Effective Teaching and Instruction

Component	Principle
Planning	Decide What to Teach Decide How to Teach Communicate Realistic Expectations
Managing	Prepare for Instruction Use Time Productively Establish Positive Environments
Delivering	Present Information Monitor Presentations Adjust Presentations
Evaluating	Monitor Student Understanding Monitor Engaged Time Keep Records of Student Progress Use Data to Make Decisions

SOURCE: Algozzine, Ysseldyke, & Elliott (1997)

Example of Key Aspects of Model Underlying Structure of Our Book

Component	Principle	Strategy
Planning	Decide What to Teach	Assess to Identify Gaps in Performance Establish Logical Sequences of Instruction Consider Contextual Variables
	Decide How to Teach	Set Instructional Goals Establish Performance Standards Choose Instructional Methods and Materials Establish Grouping Structures Pace Instruction Appropriately Monitor Performance and Replan Instruction
	Communicate Realistic Expectations	Teach Goals, Objectives, and Standards Teach Students to Be Active, Involved Learners Teach Students Consequences of Performance

SOURCE: Algozzine, Ysseldyke, & Elliott (1997)

Organizational Relations in Algozzine and Ysseldyke Model	
Component:	Delivering Instruction
Principle:	Monitor Presentations
Strategy:	Provide Prompts and Cues
Tactic:	*Use Signals to Request Help:* Develop a signal for each student to use when assistance is needed during an independent practice session. Circulate through the room when students are practicing and look for signs that someone needs help. Provide help as quickly as possible so that students can continue to work.

SOURCE: Algozzine, Ysseldyke, & Elliott (1997)

Algozzine and Ysseldyke (1992) and Algozzine et al. (1997) used the model as a base for a collection of evidence-based tactics to help teachers teach more effectively. In *63 Tactics for Teaching Diverse Learners, Grades 6–12*, we have compiled additional tactics drawn from review of professional publications and from extensive observations of experienced teachers and other professionals who teach students with disabilities and diverse learning needs in general education classrooms. We grouped them according to the components and principles of effective instruction identified by Algozzine and Ysseldyke (see below).

Components, Principles, and Strategies for Effective Instruction

Component	Principle	Strategy
Planning Instruction	Decide What to Teach	Assess to Identify Gaps in Performance Establish Logical Sequences of Instruction Consider Contextual Variables

Component	Principle	Strategy
	Decide How to Teach	Set Instructional Goals Establish Performance Standards Choose Instructional Methods and Materials Establish Grouping Structures Pace Instruction Appropriately Monitor Performance and Replan Instruction
	Communicate Realistic Expectations	Teach Goals, Objectives, and Standards Teach Students to Be Active, Involved Learners Teach Students Consequences of Performance
Managing Instruction	Prepare for Instruction	Set Classroom Rules Communicate and Teach Classroom Rules Communicate Consequences of Behavior Handle Disruptions Efficiently Teach Students to Manage Their Own Behavior
	Use Time Productively	Establish Routines and Procedures Organize Physical Space Allocate Sufficient Time to Academic Activities
	Establish Positive Classroom Environments	Make the Classroom a Pleasant, Friendly Place Accept Individual Differences Establish Supportive, Cooperative Learning Environments Create a Nonthreatening Learning Environment
Delivering Instruction	Present Information	*Presenting Content* Gain and Maintain Attention Review Prior Skills or Lessons Provide Organized, Relevant Lessons
		Motivating Students Show Enthusiasm and Interest Use Rewards Effectively Consider Level and Student Interest
		Teaching Thinking Skills Model Thinking Skills Teach Fact-Finding Skills Teach Divergent Thinking Teach Learning Strategies
		Providing Relevant Practice Develop Automaticity Vary Opportunities for Practice Vary Methods of Practice Monitor Amount of Work Assigned

(Continued)

(Continued)

Component	Principle	Strategy
	Monitor Presentations	*Providing Feedback* Give Immediate, Frequent, Explicit Feedback Provide Specific Praise and Encouragement Model Correct Performance Provide Prompts and Cues Check Student Understanding
		Keeping Students Actively Involved Monitor Performance Regularly Monitor Performance During Practice Use Peers to Improve Instruction Provide Opportunities for Success Limit Opportunities for Failure Monitor Engagement Rates
	Adjust Presentations	Adapt Lessons to Meet Student Needs Provide Varied Instructional Options Alter Pace
Evaluating Instruction	Monitor Student Understanding	Check Understanding of Directions Check Procedural Understanding Monitor Student Success Rate
	Monitor Engaged Time	Check Student Participation Teach Students to Monitor Their Own Participation
	Keep Records of Student Progress	Teach Students to Chart Their Own Progress Regularly Inform Students of Performance Maintain Records of Student Performance
	Use Data to Make Decisions	Use Data to Decide if More Services Are Warranted Use Student Progress to Make Teaching Decisions Use Student Progress to Decide When to Discontinue Services

SOURCE: Algozzine & Ysseldyke (1992); Algozzine, Ysseldyke, & Elliott (1997)

63 Tactics for Teaching Diverse Learners, Grades 6–12 is based on a fundamental belief: *teachers are able to respond to individual differences more effectively when provided with an easily accessible resource of effective tactics. 63 Tactics for Teaching Diverse Learners, Grades 6–12* responds to two fundamental problems in education: regardless of certification area, (1) very few teachers receive sufficient experience during student teaching or practicum experiences in identifying or using evidence-based tactics of effective instruction, and (2) very few teachers receive instruction in or have access to specific tactics for addressing instructional diversity and meeting individual needs in their classrooms.

63 Tactics for Teaching Diverse Learners, Grades 6–12 also responds to a widespread need in today's middle and secondary classrooms. Most teachers agree: they often do not have enough time to meet all the needs of all their students effectively. Thus, time is an ongoing and primary need. *63 Tactics for Teaching Diverse Learners, Grades 6–12* addresses this need by providing teachers with quick access to reliable information about effective instructional tactics, regardless of their area of expertise or the diverse needs of their students. When using the book, teachers have several options:

- Identifying a problem and searching for solutions using the model of effective instruction, grade level, content area, category of student disability, and/or type of student learning difference.
- Searching the database without referencing a problem or any aspects of it.
- Examining the knowledge base underlying each tactic.
- Saving items from the database for later use.
- Implementing tactics.
- Evaluating and revising instructional plans using information in the database.

Where to Go From Here

Teachers are faced daily with questions that must be addressed if they are to be effective with all children.

I teach students in a large urban high school. My specialty is history and mathematics. How can I develop appropriate learning activities for a student with learning disabilities? How can I arrange my instruction to accommodate students with a deficit in short-term memory? How can I improve my ongoing assessment of student learning? How do I use data to make decisions?

63 Tactics for Teaching Diverse Learners, Grades 6–12 helps teachers to associate a problem with an easily accessible set of solutions. It helps teachers move from questions to answers in a rapid and organized manner. It is unique in that we not only provide classroom-tested tactics for effective instruction for students with disabilities, but we also substantiate them with relevant and related literature. Thus, teachers can be assured of implementing evidence-based practices grounded in ongoing research. We also provide feedback, comments, and examples from practicing teachers who offer practical suggestions as to how the tactic might be modified and/or enhanced in terms of its content or application.

Acknowledgments

No one writes a book without help and support from others, and we are no exception. When we began this project, our goal was to share what we had learned from working with teachers and their students around the country. We are thankful for that experience and for what they and our own students continually taught us. We are also grateful to our colleagues, who by way of conducting and reporting their research have provided an ever-renewing resource of evidence-based practices for helping diverse learners to succeed in school. We also acknowledge the very professional support of David Chao, Brynn Saito, and Kathleen McLane at Corwin; they kept us on track and contributed greatly to every part of producing this book.

Corwin gratefully acknowledges the contributions of the following individuals:

Scott Currier
Mathematics Teacher
Belmont High School
Belmont, NH

Randy Wormald
Math teacher, Grades 9–12
Belmont High School
Belmont, NH

About the Authors

 **Bob Algozzine,** PhD, from Penn State University, is codirector of the Behavior and Reading Improvement Center and professor of educational administration, research, and technology at the University of North Carolina at Charlotte. He is the coauthor of *Strategies and Tactics for Effective Instruction, Critical Issues in Special and Remedial Education, Introduction to Special Education, 63 Tactics for Teaching Diverse Learners, K–6,* and other college textbooks. He has published more than 250 articles on effective teaching, assessment, special education issues, and improving the lives of individuals with disabilities. His recent research has been published in the *High School Journal,* the *Journal of Educational Research,* and *Teacher Education and Special Education.* He has been a special education classroom teacher and college professor for more than 30 years in public schools and universities in New York, Virginia, Pennsylvania, Florida, and North Carolina. For nine years, he was coeditor, with Martha Thurlow, of *Exceptional Children,* the premiere research journal in the field of special education. He is currently the coeditor of *Teacher Education and Special Education,* the *Journal of Special Education,* and *Career Development for Exceptional Individuals.*

 **Pam Campbell,** PhD, from the University of Florida, is an associate professor in the Department of Special Education at the University of Nevada–Las Vegas (UNLV). During her 35 years as an educator, she has taught university courses in instruction, assessment, curriculum, and classroom management for both general and special educators. In addition, she has been a public school teacher in general education, Chapter I, and special education classrooms. She served in the dual role of university professor and coordinator of seven Professional Development Schools (PDS) at the University of Connecticut and currently serves at UNLV as coordinator of the Paradise PDS. Her research interests focus on linking the preparation of teacher candidates and sustained professional development of practicing teachers through technology. Her work has been published in *TEACHING Exceptional Children, Remedial and Special Education, Record in Educational Leadership,* the *Professional Educator,* and the *Council for Administrators of Special Education* (now the *Journal of Special Education Leadership*). She is also the coauthor of *Improving Social Competence: Techniques for Elementary Teachers* and *63 Tactics for Teaching Diverse Learners, K–6.* She has served the field of special education through numerous local, state, regional, and national presentations and as field reviewer for *Exceptional Children,* the *Journal of Special Education Technology, TEACHING Exceptional Children,* and *Teacher Education and Special Education.*

 **Jianjun (Adam) Wang,** MA from University of Connecticut, is senior instructional technology specialist at Williams College. He has been responsible for collaborating with Campbell, Algozzine, and James Ysseldyke in the design and development of STRIDE, a database program that provided the framework for the contents of this book. In addition, he has coauthored (with Algozzine and Campbell) *63 Tactics for Teaching Diverse Learners, K–6*. He has also been instrumental in the implementation of STRIDE in the preparation of future teachers, as well as the ongoing professional development of practicing educators. He has served as an instructor in technology courses and made several regional, national, and international conference presentations related to the effective implementation of technology in education. His research interests concern how educational technology can enhance human learning and focus on developing Web-based learning and teaching tools to enhance the undergraduate learning experience.

Planning Instruction

Effective teachers carefully plan their instruction. They decide what to teach and how to teach it. They also communicate their expectations for learning to their students. In this part of our resource, we describe evidenced-based strategies for each principle of planning instruction.

Component	Principle	Strategy
Planning Instruction (Part I)	Decide What to Teach (Chapter 1)	Assess to Identify Gaps in Performance Establish Logical Sequences of Instruction Consider Contextual Variables
	Decide How to Teach (Chapter 2)	Set Instructional Goals Establish Performance Standards Choose Instructional Methods and Materials Establish Grouping Structures Pace Instruction Appropriately Monitor Performance and Replan Instruction
	Communicate Realistic Expectations (Chapter 3)	Teach Goals, Objectives, and Standards Teach Students to Be Active, Involved Learners Teach Students Consequences of Performance

Planning Instruction Works: A Case Study

I've always considered myself an excellent planner, regardless of the fact that my principal reviews my plan book every Friday. I really want to be organized and prepared; you know, you have to be with 35 ninth graders in one room. So I've been very careful in deciding what and how to teach; I also know exactly what the instructional goals and objectives are each day. I have collaborated with our special education staff to ensure that each student's Individualized Educational Plan (IEP) includes appropriate instructional goals and objectives that specify exactly how each objective will be taught and measured. The IEPs use the ABCC format: Actor (the student), Behavior (observable/measurable student action), Content (materials/methods used), and Criterion (how student performance will be measured). For example: "Given 10 flashcards, John will able to name 10 CVC [consonant-vowel-consonant; e.g., h-a-t] words with 90 percent accuracy." So this year, it has been so helpful to have Mr. Laird, my special education co-teacher, in my classroom for most of the day. Between the two of us, we are able to circulate around the classroom and really monitor and record student learning, as well as respond to any questions or problems students might be having. When we compare our notes, we are able to make accurate decisions about what and how to teach the next day. It's really great because not only are we able to make immediate modifications for any of our students, we can be really smart about planning next steps and ensure that we're adhering to IEPs. We are also really able to "close the loop" between evaluating and planning instruction. (Related tactic is located in Chapter 2: Decide How to Teach under Strategy: Monitor Performance and Replan Instruction.)

1

Decide What to Teach

Component	Principle	Strategy
Planning Instruction	Decide What to Teach	Assess to Identify Gaps in Performance Establish Logical Sequences of Instruction Consider Contextual Variables

Chapter 1: Decide What to Teach

Strategy:	**Assess to Identify Gaps in Performance**

Content Skills:	Mathematics/Problem Solving/Calculating; Reading
Learning Difference:	Cognition Low; Attention; Processing Visual Information; Receptive Language/Decoding (listening, reading); Fine Motor (handwriting, articulation, etc.); Processing Verbal Information; Expressive Language/ Encoding (speaking, writing, spelling); Cognition Mixed
Disability Category:	Specific Learning Disabilities; Mental Retardation; Speech or Language Impairments; Serious Emotional Disturbance; Attention Deficit/Hyperactivity Disorder; Autism; Gifted and Talented; Hearing Impairments; Multiple Disabilities; Traumatic Brain Injury; Visual Impairments; Deafness/Blindness; Orthopedic Impairments; Other Health Impairments

Tactic Title:	**Think-Aloud Problem Solving**

Problem:	Teachers often think that if they knew more about the way students were thinking and reasoning, they would be better equipped to evaluate students' understanding of problem-solving methods.
Tactic:	When evaluating problem-solving or reasoning skills of students (especially in mathematics), take students aside individually and have them describe what they are doing as they work through word problems. Tell them to say exactly what they are thinking and doing. Keep careful records of their verbalizations. (A tape recorder is helpful for this purpose.) The think-aloud procedure can be used alone or as a component of a unit test. After the evaluation is complete, review the strategies that students used to arrive at their solutions.
Example:	I've found this tactic to be very helpful because I can see exactly where a student is going astray in thinking and start reteaching at that point. In fact, the students often show me an excellent alternative to my own thinking. Sometimes, when my time is limited, I've organized the students into dyads and let them talk through their thinking with a peer . . . [a] nice way to include students of differing abilities in shared problem-solving. For those students who have expressive languages issues, I've found that just observing their work closely provides extremely useful information for me, as the teacher. While I've used this idea in my algebra and general mathematics classes, I'm sure teachers in other content areas would find it very useful.

Arturo C., teacher

Benefits: Verbalizing thinking enables teachers to

- design instruction that is specific to the exact needs and abilities of students;
- incorporate opportunities for students to use their strategies on tests; and
- ensure that individual learning styles, appropriate modifications, and IEP objectives are being met.

Literature: Marjorie, M., & Applegate, B. (1993). Middle school students' mathematical problem solving: An analysis of think-aloud protocols. *Learning Disability Quarterly, 16,* 19–30.

Chapter 1: Decide What to Teach

Strategy:	**Establish Logical Sequences of Instruction**

Content Skills: Mathematics/Problem Solving/Calculating; Reading; Writing; Social Studies; Science; Arts; Music

Learning Difference: Self-Confidence; Social Knowledge; Social Behaviors; Expressive Language/Encoding (speaking, writing, spelling)

Disability Category: Specific Learning Disabilities; Autism; Orthopedic Impairments; Other Health Impairments; Attention Deficit/Hyperactivity Disorder; Speech or Language Impairments; Specific Learning Disabilities; Serious Emotional Disturbance; Hearing Impairments; Mental Retardation; Multiple Disabilities; Traumatic Brain Injury; Visual Impairments; Deafness/Blindness; Gifted and Talented

Tactic Title:	**Assessing Student Participation in Group Activities**

Problem: When teachers ask questions in a group setting, most students will volunteer answers some of the time. However, other students may hesitate to respond due to shyness, lack of confidence or knowledge, and/or misunderstanding the question. Consequently, teachers may not be able to assess what these students really know.

Tactic: To encourage greater participation, first ask a question to the class as a whole. Select students who raise their hands and thank them for participating. Provide supportive and/or corrective feedback. Then, ask additional questions; however, select students who do not raise their hands as well. Encourage any response (related to the question) and, again, acknowledge participation and provide supportive/corrective feedback. Pay attention to the quieter students to ensure that you notice when they do raise their hands. Be sure that students know why it is important to participate, even if they are not sure of their responses.

Example: With more and more students with disabilities being included in my classes, it is essential that I make every effort to encourage them to participate. Some are really hesitant . . . at first, because they may not know the other students in the class and, then, because they are not sure of the content. Some are simply shy; they like to listen. However, I've always tried to create a community of learners that accepts others abilities and disabilities; it just makes the conversations so much richer. I make sure that I ask a variety of questions, both open- and closed-ended and at different levels of Bloom's taxonomy. In fact, I keep a "Bloom's Guide" with me most of the time when I'm teaching; it's invaluable. Sometimes during class discussions, I divide the students into two groups and monitor their participation as a group. Now, so many students volunteer that it sometimes hard to keep track of it all.

Emma F., teacher

Benefits: Using this tactic will

- encourage all students, including those with disabilities, to participate more often;
- demonstrate to the entire class that everyone's participation is valued; and
- give teachers more data with which to assess student understanding and learning.

Literature: Henderson, H. A., & Fox, N. (1998). Inhibited and uninhibited children: Challenges in school settings. *School Psychology Review, 27,* 492–505.

Chapter 1: Decide What to Teach

Strategy:	**Consider Contextual Variables**
Content Skills:	Mathematics/Problem Solving/Calculating; Reading; Writing; Social Studies; Science; Arts; Music
Learning Difference:	Cognition Low; Attention; Processing Visual Information; Receptive Language/Decoding (listening, reading); Fine Motor (handwriting, articulation, etc.); Processing Verbal Information; Expressive Language/ Encoding (speaking, writing, spelling); Cognition Mixed
Disability Category:	Specific Learning Disabilities; Mental Retardation; Speech or Language Impairments; Serious Emotional Disturbance; Attention Deficit/ Hyperactivity Disorder; Autism; Gifted and Talented; Hearing Impairments; Multiple Disabilities; Traumatic Brain Injury; Visual Impairments; Deafness/Blindness; Orthopedic Impairments; Other Health Impairments

Tactic Title:	**Mapping Your Classroom**
Problem:	Deciding what to teach involves much more than just the content. Teachers are constantly monitoring the "atmosphere" of their classrooms to arrange the context to ensure opportunities for student learning. Determining which students work most effectively with one another is critical; otherwise, learning may be disrupted by off-task behavior, friction among students, or lack of motivation.
Tactic:	Give each student a class list with three columns (see Grouping Chart Part I) to indicate which students they would like to work with: 1 = Very Much; 2 = OK; 3 = Preferably Not. Assure the students that their responses are confidential and that you will use the information for grouping purposes only. Use another grid with students' names entered in alphabetical order horizontally and vertically (see Grouping Chart Part II). Starting with the first student in the vertical column, enter each student's rankings across the page. Total responses horizontally and vertically. When you have finished, you will have a clear "picture," a map, of your students' preferences and groups of students that might work well together.
Example:	I've used a similar sociometric tool for years and found it invaluable in "taking the temperature" of my classroom. It's important to repeat the assessment several times during the school year, as student relationships are constantly changing. I realize that standard seating arrangements may be necessary in some situations (testing, homeroom, music, etc.). However, when grouping students is appropriate, giving them some say really seems to increase their motivation.

Denny S., teacher

Benefits: Sociometric tools enable

- students to express their learning preferences;
- teachers to gauge interpersonal relationships and grouping preferences to facilitate student learning; and
- greater student involvement in determining the contexts for their
  learning.

Literature: Campbell, P., & Siperstein, G. (1994). *Improving social competence:
                                  A resource for elementary school teachers.* Boston: Allyn & Bacon.

Grouping Chart (Part 1)

Directions: List student names alphabetically in **Student Names** column. Ask students to select one of the three choices (Very Much, OK, Preferably No) to choose peers with whom they would like to collaborate. Give one sheet to each student in the class.

Student Names	1 *Very Much*	2 *OK*	3 *Preferably No*

Grouping Chart (Part 2)

Directions: Enter student names in Column 1 (vertically) and Row 1 (horizontally) in alphabetical order. Using individual student worksheets (Part 1), begin with Student 1 in Column 1. Working horizontally, enter that student's ratings (1–3) for all classmates (from left to right). Note: There will be no ratings entered in the box that corresponds vertically and horizontally for a particular student. Total ratings horizontally to see what one student thinks about others. Total ratings vertically to see what other students think about a student. Review totals carefully to determine which students would work together well, which students need a classmate who would be willing to work with them, and which students are willing to work with others. Repeat this assessment periodically as relationships change.

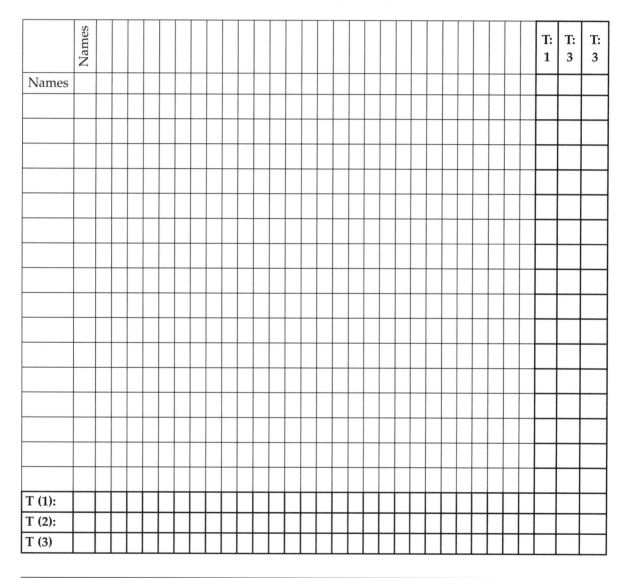

2

Decide How to Teach

Principle	Strategy
Decide How to Teach	Set Instructional Goals
	Establish Performance Standards
	Choose Instructional Methods and Materials
	Establish Grouping Structures
	Pace Instruction Appropriately
	Monitor Performance and Replan Instruction

Chapter 2: Decide How to Teach

Strategy:	Set Instructional Goals

Content Skills:	Arts; Fitness; Mathematics/Problem Solving/Calculating; Reading; Social Studies; Science; Writing
Learning Difference:	Cognition Low; Fine Motor (handwriting, articulation, etc.); Expressive Language/Encoding (speaking, writing, spelling); Receptive Language/Decoding (listening, reading); Attention; Cognition High; Mobility; Hearing; Health; Cognition Mixed; Memory Short-Term; Memory Long-Term; Seeing; Speaking/Talking; Study Skills; Gross Motor (running, walking, etc.); Processing Visual Information; Processing Verbal Information; Social Knowledge; Self-Control; Social Behaviors; Self-Confidence; Self-Care
Disability Category:	Mental Retardation; Visual Impairments; Deafness/Blindness; Gifted and Talented; Hearing Impairments; Multiple Disabilities; Traumatic Brain Injury; Serious Emotional Disturbance; Specific Learning Disabilities; Speech or Language Impairments; Attention Deficit/Hyperactivity Disorder; Orthopedic Impairments; Other Health Impairments; Autism

Tactic Title:	Using Portfolios to Report Student Learning
Problem:	Assessing the performance of students with disabilities is challenging, as they have unique learning styles, specific instructional needs (including assessment), and varying degrees of success with expressive language (particularly in written work).
Tactic:	First, review some of the student's work and find areas of strength and areas that need improvement. Together with the special education teacher, develop specific instructional goals for the student (if he or she does not have an Individualized Educational Plan, or IEP); you might use the following Goals/Objectives Planning Worksheet. Maintain a portfolio of student work to be reviewed as frequently as possible. Look for areas of improvement or attainment of goals and share your observations with the student. Encourage the student to assume this responsibility over time. As students meet current goals and objectives, develop new expectations.
Example:	Portfolios are a wonderful supplement to report cards; they are also an important component in parent conferences, collaborating with special educators, and IEP meetings. I review every student's portfolio weekly and have a five-minute conference with the student. Oftentimes, we are able to identify specific skills that need remediation. I've always let my students develop a supplemental portfolio of work that they select for inclusion. They must also include a rationale for including

a particular piece. I send these portfolios home with students periodically to be signed by parents; it's a nice way to communicate good news to parents.

Luisa F., teacher

Benefits: Portfolios are an excellent tool because they

- provide a way for teachers to see if a student is improving in several areas after instruction has taken place;
- can demonstrate student successes that may not be reflected in traditional reporting methods; and
- serve as a tool for communicating with other professionals, parents, and individual students.

Literature: Siegel-Causey, E., & Allinger, R. M. (1998). Using alternative assessment for students with severe disabilities: Alignment with best practices. *Education and Training in Mental Retardation and Developmental Disabilities, 33,* 168–175.

Goals/Objectives Planning Worksheet

Date/Period:	Goals/Objectives:	Meeting Date:	Comments:

Chapter 2: Decide How to Teach

Strategy:	**Establish Performance Standards**
Learning Difference:	Cognition High; Processing Verbal Information; Receptive Language/Decoding (listening, reading); Expressive Language/Encoding (speaking, writing, spelling); Processing Visual Information
Disability Category:	Gifted and Talented

Tactic Title:	**Compacting the Curriculum**
Problem:	Many students are classified as having gifts and talents in several or specific areas. Such students include those with learning disabilities, emotional disturbance, and several other categories of disability that do not involve cognitive impairments. These students are often not sufficiently academically challenged, and their learning is affected.
Tactic:	Students who know and understand a particular curriculum should not be required to learn information that they already know. Compact information and curriculum for students with high ability levels; teach only the content that they need to learn. Provide these students with enrichment opportunities that will challenge them. Students will not have "more" work; their assignments will just be different and more advanced and appropriate for their needs.
Example:	This is not difficult to accomplish. As my classes have become more diversified, I've learned to readjust my thinking that "one approach/content fits all". . . simply not true. Finding varied ways to meet instructional goals and objectives is certainly challenging; however, I have found that the motivation of my students to learn has increased exponentially. Find the specialists in your building who can provide the ideas and materials that you need. Also, there are excellent resources online . . . journals, Web sites, etc. *Marissa A., teacher*
Benefits:	When teachers adjust their curriculum and instruction for students for any student, • students are challenged and more motivated to learn and participate; • all classmates benefit from the enrichment of the curriculum; and • teachers see that achievement scores and acceptance of learning differences improve.
Literature:	Reis, S. M., & Renzulli, J. S. (1992). Using curriculum compacting to challenge the above-average. *Educational Leadership, 50,* 51–57. Renzulli, J. S., & Reis, S. M. (1998). Talent development through curriculum differentiation. *NASSP Bulletin, 82,* 61–74.

Chapter 2: Decide How to Teach

Strategy:	**Choose Instructional Methods and Materials**
Content Skills:	Arts; Fitness; Mathematics/Problem Solving/Calculating; Reading; Social Studies; Science; Writing
Learning Difference:	Speaking/Talking; Receptive Language/Decoding (listening, reading); Processing Verbal Information; Processing Verbal Information; Expressive Language/Encoding (speaking, writing, spelling); Social Knowledge; Social Behaviors; Self-Confidence; Processing Visual Information; Study Skills; Cognition Mixed
Disability Category:	Speech or Language Impairments; Specific Learning Disabilities; Serious Emotional Disturbance; Mental Retardation; Traumatic Brain Injury

Tactic Title:	**Accommodating Students With Second Language Needs (EL/ELL)**
Problem:	Students with language processing disabilities or those whose native language is not English often have difficulty understanding directions and the content of materials presented in secondary classrooms. As a result, they may become frustrated when they are unable to comprehend lessons or communicate effectively with their teachers or classmates.
Tactic:	First, ensure that students with a language processing/learning issue have the services of a specialist. Second, in consultation with the specialist(s), deliver instructions (both oral and written) in students' native languages and with appropriate gloss notes to provide additional directions. Gloss notes include highlighted/bulleted/bold text to emphasize important points. Provide computer programs and other technological tools to assist students. Finally, expose students to as much appropriate oral and written English language and give them as many opportunities to practice using English appropriately as possible.
Example:	All too often I have seen teachers basically ignore these students because they are not sure how to teach them. This was always very disturbing to me. I do agree that they need isolated time with a specialist who can increase their ability to understand and use the English language. However, it is not enough for them to simply be taken out of the classroom to work with a specialist. These students really just need every possible opportunity to be around others who use the English language appropriately. The classroom is their community, and everything possible should be done to make them feel welcome. I have found through my own experience that these students learn English with the least amount of anxiety and difficulty when they can relate what is being said in the classroom to their homework, thereby strengthening their knowledge of both their vernacular and English. I am highly

supportive of giving ESL students written assignments in their native language whenever possible. I also make it a point to discuss with other students the fact that non-English-speaking students need support and friends as much as they do. It is also important to give visual aids along with verbal instruction.

Jesse I., teacher

Benefits: When classroom teachers accommodate the needs of students with English-language learning needs,

- students become more involved in daily classroom activities;
- appropriate social interactions increase; and
- self-esteem and academic achievement improve.

Literature: Chang, A. C.-S., & Read, J. (2008). Reducing listening test anxiety through various forms of listening support. *TESL-EJ, 12*(1), 1–25.

Chapter 2: Decide How to Teach

Strategy:	**Establish Grouping Structures**
Content Skills:	Mathematics/Problem Solving/Calculating
Learning Difference:	Memory Long-Term; Cognition Mixed; Processing Visual Information; Expressive Language/Encoding (speaking, writing, spelling); Processing Verbal Information; Study Skills
Disability Category:	Specific Learning Disabilities; Traumatic Brain Injury; Serious Emotional Disturbance; Speech or Language Impairments; Attention Deficit/ Hyperactivity Disorder; Autism

Tactic Title:	**Using Student Interests to Teach Problem Solving**
Problem:	Students often have trouble with problem solving, especially in mathematics.
Tactic:	First, focus on a topic/problem that students want to explore, such as creating a skateboarding ramp. Next, create a multilevel problem that the students have to solve that includes the math and problem-solving skills being taught. Before presenting the problem to the students, review background knowledge with them that they will need to work on the problem. Then, separate the class into groups of three to five students. After students are assigned to groups, present the problem to them as a class. Let the students discover, in their groups, how to tackle the problem; they might use the following Problem-Solving Worksheet to organize their thinking and work through the problem. Provide support if a group is having difficulty, such as not considering a certain approach. Finally, have the groups report their findings to classmates.
Example:	I've found that when I begin planning from where my students "are" in terms of their interests/concerns, it's so much easier to motivate and involve them in problem-solving activities. They are so much more excited about assignments; also, my concerns regarding time-on-task are minimized because they are so involved. Finally, I'm able to arrange small groups of students with diverse needs. . . . This really helps with the interpersonal relationships as well. *Jake R., teacher*
Benefits:	Using student interests as the basis for teaching problem solving strategies • is applicable across content areas, disabilities, and grade levels; • keeps students interested and involved; and • takes advantages of a student's inclination to explore problems that are contextualized and, therefore, have meaning.
Literature:	Bottage, B. A. (1999). Effects of contextualized math instruction on problem solving on average and below-average achieving students. *Journal of Special Education, 33,* 81–92.

Problem-Solving Worksheet

Problem:

_____

_____

_____

_____

Hypothesis:

_____

_____

Steps to solve problem:

_____   _____

_____   _____

_____   _____

_____   _____

_____   _____

_____   _____

Solution:

_____

_____

_____

_____

_____

Chapter 2: Decide How to Teach

Strategy:	Pace Instruction Appropriately
Content Skills:	Science
Learning Difference:	Cognition Low; Attention; Study Skills; Processing Verbal Information; Processing Visual Information
Disability Category:	Specific Learning Disabilities; Attention Deficit/Hyperactivity Disorder; Serious Emotional Disturbance; Mental Retardation; Traumatic Brain Injury; Speech or Language Impairments; Autism

Tactic Title:	Using Discovery Learning to Teach the Differences Between Plant and Animal Cells
Problem:	Students often have difficulty understanding the differences between plant and animal cells.
Tactic:	After discussing the differences between plant and animal cells, ask students to draw what they think these cells would look like under a microscope. After they complete the drawings, allow students to prepare microscope slides of plant (onion) and animal (skin scraping) cells. Then tell students to view the slides they have prepared and make drawings of the plant and animal cells they see through the microscope next to those they had previously drawn. Ask students to label structures in their second set of drawings, using their textbook as a reference, and then compare and contrast the two types of cells. Then question students to determine whether their understanding of the material is more comprehensive than before the exercise. Students should be able to discern the characteristic structures of plant and animal cells easily after the exercise.
Example:	This tactic demonstrates the importance of using realia as well as abstract methods of instruction. I've found that simply lecturing content to students is not always enough. Students need not only to "hear" about content; they also need to be engaged in a real-life example of the abstract content. I've always tried to find ways to make the required content "real" and "meaningful" for my students. It's not always easy, but it has really helped students achieve greater results in my classes.

Diane St. P., teacher

Benefits:	This tactic allows students to

- express their preconceived notions;
- see whether their preconceived notions were correct or not;
- discover this information for themselves; and
- become open to conceptual change because they proved it to themselves.

Literature:	Dalton, B., Morocco, C., Tivnan, T., & Mead, P. R. (1997). Supported inquiry science: Teaching for conceptual change in urban and suburban science classrooms. *Journal of Learning Disabilities, 30,* 670–684.

Chapter 2: Decide How to Teach

Strategy:	**Monitor Performance and Replan Instruction**

Content Skills:	Writing; Social Studies; Science; Reading; Mathematics/Problem Solving/Calculating; Fitness; Arts
Learning Difference:	Speaking/Talking; Expressive Language/Encoding (speaking, writing, spelling); Attention; Hearing; Cognition Low; Mobility; Cognition High; Health; Cognition Mixed; Memory Short-Term; Memory Long-Term; Seeing; Study Skills; Fine Motor (handwriting, articulation, etc.); Gross Motor (running, walking, etc.); Processing Visual Information; Processing Verbal Information; Receptive Language/Decoding (listening, reading); Social Knowledge; Self-Control; Social Behaviors; Self-Confidence; Self-Care
Disability Category:	Specific Learning Disabilities; Visual Impairments; Deafness/Blindness; Gifted and Talented; Hearing Impairments; Mental Retardation; Multiple Disabilities; Traumatic Brain Injury; Serious Emotional Disturbance; Speech or Language Impairments; Attention Deficit/Hyperactivity Disorder; Orthopedic or Other Health Impairments; Autism

Tactic Title:	**Monitoring and Planning Appropriately**

Problem:	Teachers often find it challenging to know what students with disabilities have learned and what should come next in terms of instruction due to a discrepancy between expected and actual achievement.
Tactic:	Use both written and verbal assessments to allow all students to excel in areas of strength and map their progress in weaker areas. Incorporate these assessments into individual portfolios. Explain to them that it is a great way for everyone to monitor their progress and plan for subsequent learning. Include written assignments and tape recording (video/audio) of oral assignments. Next, provide criteria for students as to how to select items for their portfolio. They should be aware that not everything should be included. For each entry selected, they should write a brief description as to why they believe it is representative of their learning. Explain to students how to assess their own learning and how it links their prior learning to present learning. Finally, invite parents, students, and colleagues to a "Portfolio Night" where students can share their achievements with others. Students should prepare to explain each entry, how/why it is representative of their progress, why each entry is important to them, and what it indicates in terms of future learning for them.
Example:	I've used portfolios for years in collaboration with my special education teacher to help us monitor student learning and plan on a continual basis. . . . We meet at least once a week, regardless, to review the

achievements of our students. Then, together with students and parents, we are able to make the most appropriate instructional decisions.

Drew P., teacher

Benefits: Using portfolios as a supplement to traditional and required assessments

- strengthens the voice of students within the assessment process, because they have a say in what they believe is representative of their learning and what they need;
- enables teachers, parents, and students to collaborate in reviewing achievements and planning future goals/objectives together; and
- heightens students' awareness and commitment to critical assessment of their learning.

Literature: Herbert, E., & Schultz, L. (1996). The power of portfolios. *Educational Leadership, 53*(7), 70–71.

3

Communicate Realistic Expectations

Principle	Strategy
Communicate Realistic Expectations	Teach Goals, Objectives, and Standards
	Teach Students to Be Active, Involved Learners
	Teach Students Consequences of Performance

Chapter 3: Communicate Realistic Expectations

Strategy:	**Teach Goals, Objectives, and Standards**
Content Skills:	Arts; Fitness; Mathematics/Problem Solving/Calculating; Reading; Social Studies; Science; Writing
Learning Difference:	Attention; Self-Control; Social Behaviors; Self-Confidence
Disability Category:	Attention Deficit/Hyperactivity Disorder (ADHD)

Tactic Title:	**Rewards and Punishments: Promoting Positive Reinforcement**
Problem:	Students with ADHD and those with other disabilities often find the structure and expectations of general education classrooms challenging. In addition, they deal with multiple teaching styles across several classroom settings.
Tactic:	Together with the student, develop a contract to promote appropriate behavior. Determine the specific behaviors that are desired and the incentives that will be provided to the student. Incentives are appropriate "rewards" that the *student* wants and are related to learning. Incentives might include working with a peer, using the computer, "free" reading time, etc. Then set a date for renegotiating the contract; sign and date the contract. The Contract Worksheet that follows can be modified for students to obtain daily signatures from all teachers.
Example:	I've used behavior contract with many of my special education students. They keep the contracts in their assignment notebooks and carry them from class to class, where each teacher signs off on appropriate behavior throughout the day. I also require my students to obtain a parent signature and return it to me before school the following day. It's a really nice way to provide some consistency across very different classroom settings and teachers . . . especially for students who lack self-discipline or have difficulty with change. *Ryan L., special education teacher*
Benefits:	Using positive incentives and behavior contract to promote on-task behavior • provides consistency across classrooms; • provides structure and clear expectations for students; and • gives students greater opportunities for success.
Literature:	National Institute of Mental Health (NIMH). (2004). National Institute of Mental Health multimodal treatment study of ADHD follow-up: 24-month outcomes of treatment strategies for attention-deficit/hyperactivity disorder. *Pediatrics, 113,* 754–761.

Student Behavior Contract Sheet

(Student Name)

I will behave in the following ways:

_____

_____

_____

_____

_____

My incentive will be:

_____

_____

_____

_____

This contract will be renegotiated on:

_____

_____   _____

Student Signature   **Teacher Signature**

_____   _____

Today's Date   **Today's Date**

Chapter 3: Communicate Realistic Expectations

Strategy:	**Teach Students to Be Active, Involved Learners**
Content Skills:	Arts; Fitness; Mathematics/Problem Solving/Calculating; Reading; Social Studies; Science; Writing
Learning Difference:	Cognition High; Cognition Low; Cognition Mixed; Attention; Study Skills; Processing Verbal Information; Self-Confidence; Receptive Language/Decoding (listening, reading); Expressive Language/Encoding (speaking, writing, spelling); Fine Motor (handwriting, articulation, etc.)
Disability Category:	Attention Deficit/Hyperactivity Disorder

Tactic Title:	**Making Learning Real**
Problem:	Students with disabilities are often "disconnected" from the content of their curriculum, either due to their disability or lack of interest, background knowledge, or skill. Consequently, they are less likely to participate or even try.
Tactic:	First, immerse students in the content to be taught. For example, before a poetry writing assignment, give students time to read as many poems of their choice to get a feel for the work. Before a lab, show students a real-life example. Then demonstrate what it is students need to accomplish. Be a model. Tell students what you expect them to do and then hand over responsibility to them. Require students to finish assignments in a timely manner while allowing them time to try out different strategies. Finally, have students use or employ what they are learning so they begin to understand that what they are doing is important and useful to them. For example, students could publish poetry or give it to family members. Remember to provide ongoing feedback and support during the lesson.
Example:	I really like Mr. Tierney's algebra class. He always makes what we're learning important to us in some way. For example, last week we were working on factoring quadratic equations, and he showed us how it related to calculating area. Then we built real models using different equations. I wish my other teachers would make our assignments real, too. *Marissa R., student*
Benefits:	When teachers make learning applicable to students' lives and provide multiple ways of learning, students • become more engaged, even with a disability; • take greater responsibility for completing assignments; and • realize that succeeding in school has meaning.
Literature:	Meeks, L. L. (1999). Making English classrooms happier places to learn. *English Journal, 88,* 73–79.

Chapter 3: Communicate Realistic Expectations

Strategy:	**Teach Students Consequences of Performance**
Content Skills:	Arts; Fitness; Mathematics/Problem Solving/Calculating; Reading; Social Studies; Science; Writing
Learning Difference:	Attention; Self-Control; Social Behaviors
Disability Category:	Attention Deficit/Hyperactivity Disorder

Tactic Title:	**Logical Consequences for Behavior**
Problem:	Frequently, students with ADHD or attention issues have difficulty paying attention. Many do not understand exactly what is expected and how consequences relate to their behavior. In addition, when they are on-task and behaving appropriately, their behavior is not usually noticed by their teachers.
Tactic:	Together with students, determine appropriate and inappropriate behaviors in your classroom and make consequences clear. When students are having difficulty paying attention and controlling their behavior, speak with the students as soon as possible and remind them of the logical consequences for their actions. Equally as important, when students are on-task and behaving appropriately, tell them that you have noticed and appreciate their efforts.
Example:	Sitting still for a whole period can be really hard sometimes, and most of the time, I get in trouble when I mess up. But not in my science class. It's really nice when Ms. Leavitt tells me I'm doing a good job paying attention. She doesn't make a bit deal out of it or say something in front of the whole class. She just comes by my desk and says "good work" or "you're doing fine" or something like that. *Jarrod B., student*
Benefits:	When students know the consequences of their behavior, they • monitor their own behavior more closely; • assume greater personal responsibility for their actions; and • engage in fewer inappropriate behaviors.
Literature:	Kohn, A. (1996). Beyond discipline. *Education Week, 16.* Retrieved November 11, 2008, from http://www.alfiekohn.org/teaching/edweek/discipline.htm

Managing Instruction

Effective teachers manage their instruction by preparing classrooms and learning materials to maximize the success of their students, by using instructional time productively, and by making classrooms positive learning environments. In this part of our resource, we describe evidence-based strategies for each principle of managing instruction.

Component	Principle	Strategy
Managing Instruction (Part II)	Prepare for Instruction (Chapter 4)	Set Classroom Rules
		Communicate and Teach Classroom Rules
		Communicate Consequences of Behavior
		Handle Disruptions Efficiently
		Teach Students to Manage Their Own Behavior
	Use Time Productively (Chapter 5)	Establish Routines and Procedures
		Organize Physical Space
		Allocate Sufficient Time to Academic Activities
	Establish Positive Environments (Chapter 6)	Make the Classroom a Pleasant, Friendly Place
		Accept Individual Differences
		Establish Supportive, Cooperative Learning Environments
		Create a Nonthreatening Learning Environment

Managing Instruction Works: A Case Study

As a new teacher, I quickly learned the importance of consistency and structure in a classroom. I started over 10 years ago as a high school teacher, and, of course, I wanted my classroom to be a welcoming and functional space for my students, so I kept changing schedules and rearranging the desks/furniture in the room. I also put every book, resource, and supply (markers, staplers, hole punchers, etc.) out so my students could use them. Big mistake. A recipe for chaos and lost instructional time. I had put out all of the tools that my students would be using over the next school year, but I had not demonstrated their use and the need to put them back when they were finished so they would be available for another student to use. As a result, I had hole punchers left all over the room, the pencil sharpener jammed with an eraser and a multicolor array of paper strewn from one side of the room to the other. So I learned a very important lesson. Learners, especially those with disabilities, really need things to be reliable and predictable. Changes need to be taught carefully. So I learned the hard way to establish routines and procedures and keep them consistent; also, I'm much more knowledgeable as to how to organize and, on occasion, reorganize the physical space in my classroom. (Related tactic is located in Chapter 5: Use Time Productively under Strategy: Organize Physical Space.)

Prepare for Instruction

Component	Principle	Strategy
Managing Instruction	*Prepare for Instruction*	*Strategy*
Managing Instruction	Prepare for Instruction	Set Classroom Rules
		Communicate and Teach Classroom Rules
		Communicate Consequences of Behavior
		Handle Disruptions Efficiently
		Teach Students to Manage Their Own Behavior

Chapter 4: Prepare for Instruction

Strategy:	**Set Classroom Rules**
Content Skills:	Writing; Science; Social Studies; Reading; Mathematics/Problem Solving/Calculating; Fitness; Arts
Learning Difference:	Attention; Study Skills; Social Knowledge; Self-Control; Social Behaviors; Self-Confidence; Self-Care; Cognition High; Cognition Low; Mobility; Hearing; Health; Cognition Mixed; Memory Short-Term; Memory Long-Term; Seeing; Speaking/Talking; Fine Motor (handwriting, articulation, etc.); Gross Motor (running, walking, etc.); Processing Visual Information; Processing Verbal Information; Receptive Language/Decoding (listening, reading); Expressive Language/Encoding (speaking, writing, spelling)
Disability Category:	Attention Deficit/Hyperactivity Disorder; Visual Impairments; Deafness/Blindness; Gifted and Talented; Hearing Impairments; Mental Retardation; Multiple Disabilities; Traumatic Brain Injury; Second Language Learning Needs; Serious Emotional Disturbance; Specific Learning Disabilities; Speech or Language Impairments; Orthopedic or Other Health Impairments; Autism

Tactic Title:	**Using Contracts to Improve Behavior and Learning**
Problem:	Teachers are often frustrated because they find themselves spending more time managing behavior rather than teaching. Consequently, tensions are raised, and student learning suffers.
Tactic:	Discuss areas of behavior that need improvement, such as remaining seated during a lesson or not talking out when others are talking. Other areas, which are more cognitively focused, could be thinking about a problem first and coming up with a personal solution, rather then asking a teacher for assistance every time a problem is encountered, or thinking about a response to a question or action before raising one's hand. Next, together decide on three or four of these areas that the student thinks are most important and write up a simple contract listing these areas (see Student Contract Sheet). At the end of the day, review the list together and record both positive comments and/or suggestions about each area.
Example:	Using contracts with some of my students has been so effective this year. It was hard in the beginning because I had to "give up" some of my authority in letting students choose some areas to improve. Also, it does take some time to set up individual contracts according to different needs and abilities, but Mr. Hever, the special education teacher, has been really helpful. In many cases, I have the students take their

contract home with them for their parents to sign. Bottom line: Things are much better now, and I'm actually spending more time teaching.

Delia S., teacher

Benefits: Student contracts

- give students clear guidelines for behavior;
- give parents the "good news," as well as the "bad";
- clarify expectations and consequences for everyone.

Literature: Tinzmann, M. B., Jones, B. F., Fennimore, T. F., Bakker, C. F., & Pierce, J. (1990). *What is the collaborative classroom?* Oak Brook, IL: North Central Regional Educational Laboratory (NCREL).

Student Contract Sheet

_____

Student Name)

I agree to:

_____

_____

_____

_____

_____

Incentives will be:

_____

_____

_____

_____

_____

This contract will be renegotiated on: _____

_____   _____

Student Signature   **Teacher Signature**

_____   _____

Today's Date   **Today's Date**

_____   _____

Date   **Date**

Chapter 4: Prepare for Instruction

Strategy:	**Communicate and Teach Classroom Rules**
Content Skills:	Arts; Fitness; Mathematics/Problem Solving/Calculating; Reading; Social Studies; Science; Writing
Learning Difference:	Self-Control; Social Knowledge; Social Behaviors; Attention; Cognition Low; Cognition Mixed; Memory Short-Term; Memory Long-Term; Processing Visual Information; Processing Verbal Information; Receptive Language/Decoding (listening, reading); Expressive Language/ Encoding (speaking, writing, spelling)
Disability Category:	Autism; Traumatic Brain Injury; Mental Retardation; Second Language Learning Needs; Serious Emotional Disturbance; Specific Learning Disabilities; Speech or Language Impairments; Attention Deficit/ Hyperactivity Disorder

Tactic Title:	**Reteaching Is a Good Idea**
Problem:	It is not enough simply to set classroom rules in place at the beginning of a term. Many students with disabilities simply do not have the ability to translate/operationalize a set of instructions without actual demonstrations, exemplars, and repetition.
Tactic:	Students with disabilities in particular benefit from ongoing review and demonstration/examplars. Therefore, be sure to post the rules in a visible place in your classroom. Include the guidelines on your study guides and syllabi. When designing lesson plans and activities, be sure to incorporate a review of the Classroom Rules into your Introduction/Linking section. Conduct brief reviews with demonstrations of ways to adhere to the rules (try to be positive) periodically. This may mean taking the time to have students "act out" inappropriate behaviors that do not adhere to your classroom rules and actually "see" the consequences of those actions. It is also important to demonstrate ways in which they can follow the rules successfully and realize the positive consequences of their appropriate actions. Remember to revisit the rules periodically throughout the term to ensure that students maintain their understanding.
Example:	I have at least seven different teachers every day . . . English, special ed, PE, music, history, science, math; I know there's one more . . . Spanish (my schedule rotates). They all have their own rules and ways of doing things. Sometimes, it just gets way too complicated to remember all the details, because the rules and procedures are not exactly the same every class every day. . . . Plus, a couple of my teachers keep adding new things and forgetting about the old ones. So, bottom line, I really like Mr. Matthews because he takes the time to remind us and

show us, really really show us, what we need to do. So what I'm saying is, he helps me learn because he shows me how to.

Joshlyn P., student

Benefits: Teaching and demonstrating ways to follow classroom rules periodically

- gives students clear reminders and examples of expectations for behavior and procedures;
- provides greater opportunities for students to succeed in front of their peers; and
- reduces occurrences of inappropriate behavior and disruptions to teaching and student learning.

Literature: Epstein, T., & Elias, M. (1996). To reach for the stars: How social/affective education can foster truly inclusive environments. *Phi Delta Kappan, 78,* 157–163.

Chapter 4: Planning for Instruction

Strategy:	**Communicate Consequences of Behavior**
Content Skills:	Arts; Fitness; Mathematics/Problem Solving/Calculating; Reading; Social Studies; Science; Writing
Learning Difference:	Self-Control; Social Knowledge; Social Behaviors; Attention; Cognition Low; Cognition Mixed; Memory Short-Term; Memory Long-Term; Processing Visual Information; Processing Verbal Information; Receptive Language/Decoding (Listening, Reading); Expressive Language/Encoding (speaking, writing, spelling)
Disability Category:	Autism; Traumatic Brain Injury; Mental Retardation; Second Language Learning Needs; Serious Emotional Disturbance; Specific Learning Disabilities; Speech or Language Impairments; Attention Deficit/Hyperactivity Disorder

Tactic Title:	**Using Positive Reinforcement to Emphasize Appropriate Behavior**
Problem:	Frequently, students with disabilities have difficulty distinguishing between acceptable and unacceptable social and academic behavior in the classroom.
Tactic:	As teachers, one of our goals is to increase the prevalence of positive behaviors, while decreasing the occurrences of unacceptable behavior. Using positive reinforcement and mild punishers (on occasion) provide immediate consequences of behavior to students. First, and most importantly, reinforce acceptable behaviors positively as often as possible. Examples of positive reinforcement could include "Thank you, _____, for doing your work so quietly [the behavior]," or "You listened so attentively while I was speaking [the behavior], _____; that will help you with your homework tonight [the consequence]." Keep the focus on the student and the specific behavior, and include a reason as to why the behavior is important and/or how it will help the student succeed (the consequences). Try to avoid *I* statements, such as "I like the way you . . ."; you want your students to learn to please themselves, not just you. Occasionally, you may have to use a mild punisher to deter unacceptable classroom behaviors. Examples of mild punishers are saying "*No,* it is *not* acceptable to interrupt in this classroom. You are interfering with . . . ," or "That is *not* appropriate behavior for the classroom," or the removal of a desired privilege. However, if you do use a punisher, it is extremely important to follow with positive reinforcement as soon as possible; this prevents you being perceived only as someone who punishes.
Example:	When I reinforce my students positively, they try to repeat the behavior. The key is to know the kinds of reinforcement that students want. I've used a smile, supportive comments, a personal note, and verbal

gestures to name just a few. I have to be careful to match my "praise" with the student, or it just doesn't work. Some students don't like to be singled out in front of their peers; others "soak it up." I use a Student Inventory [see following] at the beginning of each marking period to find out their likes *and* dislikes.

Becky L., teacher

Benefits: Using positive reinforcement and mild punishers appropriately

- reduces disruptions to student learning;
- emphasizes appropriate academic and social behaviors; and
- reinforces the structure and clearly defined expectations that are essential for many students with disabilities.

Literature: Metzler, C. W., Biglan, A., Rusby, J. C., & Sprague, J. R. (2001). Evaluation of a comprehensive behavior management program to improve school-wide positive behavior support. *Education & Treatment of Children, 24,* 448–480.

Student Inventory

Name:_____

Date:_____

1. If I am obeying the classroom rules and/or focused on learning, I would like you to:

2. If I am obeying the classroom rules and/or focused on learning, I do *not* want you to:

3. If I am *not* obeying the classroom rules and/or focused on learning, I do *not* want you to:

4. If I am *not* obeying the classroom rules and/or focused on learning, I would like you to:

Acceptable Behaviors:

1. _____

2. _____

3. _____

Time:	Acceptable	Unacceptable	Student/Teacher Agreement
———	———	———	———————
———	———	———	———————
———	———	———	———————
———	———	———	———————
———	———	———	———————
———	———	———	———————
———	———	———	———————
———	———	———	———————
———	———	———	———————
———	———	———	———————
———	———	———	———————
———	———	———	———————
———	———	———	———————
———	———	———	———————
———	———	———	———————
———	———	———	———————
———	———	———	———————

Chapter 4: Prepare for Instruction

Strategy:	**Handle Disruptions Efficiently**
Content Skills:	Arts; Fitness; Mathematics/Problem Solving/Calculating; Reading; Social Studies; Science; Writing
Learning Difference:	Attention; Social Knowledge; Self-Control; Social Behaviors; Study Skills; Cognition Mixed
Disability Category:	Attention Deficit/Hyperactivity Disorder; Mental Retardation; Traumatic Brain Injury; Serious Emotional Disturbance; Second Language Learning Needs; Specific Learning Disabilities; Speech or Language Impairments; Autism

Tactic Title:	**Nonverbal Promotion of On-Task Behavior**
Problem:	When a student behaves inappropriately, teaching and learning can be disrupted for everyone, including the student. Examples of inappropriate behavior may include talking out of turn, interrupting others, being out of seat, passing notes, texting classmates, talking incessantly, swearing, usng inappropriate gestures, etc.
Tactic:	One step forward in the education of students with ADHD in the classroom is to promote on-task behavior with self-confidence. First, when the student behaves inappropriately, give a discrete but serious nonverbal facial expression while continuing to conduct the class. Using hand movements and nonverbal facial expressions enables the teacher to continue teaching and students to continue learning. If the student continues to act inappropriately, walking by or standing next to the student acknowledges the student's disruption.
Example:	Nonverbal cues work! It is a great way to get my message across without singling out individual students and disrupting the flow of teaching. The power of a facial expression or physical proximity is underestimated as a classroom management technique. However, hand gestures and eye contact do not always work. So I might use nonverbal cues, such as placing a checkmark on a desk chart when the student is working well, on-task, or paying attention. Students can then "trade in" the checkmarks at the end of the period, week, or marking period for positive reinforcers that we've already agreed upon. I also use the charts as discussion starters when I meet with students individually. Several of my students are recording their "data" to track their behavior over time. *Phil R., teacher*

Benefits: Using nonverbal techniques to handle disruptions efficiently promotes a learning environment where

- individual student needs are respected and addressed;
- disruptions to teaching and learning are minimized; and
- students learn how to manage their own behavior.

Literature: Sprouse, C. A., Hall, C. W., Webster, R. E., & Bolen, L. M. (1998). Social perception in students with learning disabilities and attention deficit/hyperactivity disorder. *Journal of Nonverbal Behavior, 22,* 125–134.

Chapter 4: Prepare for Instruction

Strategy:	**Teach Students to Manage Their Own Behavior**
Content Skills:	Arts; Fitness; Mathematics/Problem Solving/Calculating; Reading; Social Studies; Science; Writing
Learning Difference:	Social Knowledge; Self-Control; Social Behaviors; Self-Confidence; Attention
Disability Category:	Serious Emotional Disturbance; Autism; Attention Deficit/Hyperactivity Disorder; Specific Learning Disabilities; Second Language Learning Needs; Traumatic Brain Injury; Mental Retardation

Tactic Title:	**Options for Students Who Need to Regroup**
Problem:	Sometimes, students with disabilities can become overwhelmed by schoolwork and classroom activities. Some react by "shutting down," others by lashing out, and some by crying. In addition to being embarrassed, their classmates may tease, ignore, or avoid them.
Tactic:	Diffusing potentially difficult situations is the goal. Meet individually with students whom you think might benefit from this tactic. Identify options for times when they may feel overwhelmed. Options might include time in a quiet corner of the classroom with a book, movement to a less intense area of the classroom to work with a peer, using a computer to complete the activity, etc. Ask the student for his or her preferences. Together, agree upon a signal that informs you that he or she needs a break. Signals might include a nonverbal gesture, a private comment, or an object. When the student feels overwhelmed, the student uses the signal *and* you acknowledge it. Be sure to agree upon a time limit if you think students might take advantage of the option. (See the following Prearranged Options contract.)
Example:	I have a new student who has just been placed in my class. Sarah has been labeled as Seriously Emotionally Disturbed. (I know we have different terms according to where we teach.) The point is that she's really timid right now and just needs some time to adjust; we've talked, and she's definitely struggling to take it all in right now. So she has a red pencil that she keeps in her book bag, and when she needs to, she either shows it to me or simply places it on her desk. Then she is free to go to the library for 15 minutes; the librarian and I have already made arrangements. Sarah knows that I expect her back within that time frame, and the librarian helps me monitor it all (together with Sarah's special education teacher). I've also talked with Sarah's other teachers so that we can be consistent throughout her day. She's a lot less stressed this week. *Mario L., teacher*

Benefits: Giving students options for managing their own behavior

- enables students to maintain their dignity in front of their peers;
- smooths the transition into new classrooms for students with disabilities; and
- enhances opportunities for learning and friendships among all students.

Literature: Gunter, P. L., Denny, R. K., Jack, S. L., Shores, R. E., & Nelson, C. M. (1993). Aversive stimuli in academic interactions between students with serious emotional disturbance and their teachers. *Behavioral Disorders, 18*(4), 265–274.

Behrmann, M. M. (1995). *Assistive technology for students with mild disabilities* (ERIC Digest E529). Reston, VA: ERIC Clearinghouse on Disabilities and Gifted Education, Council for Exceptional Children. (ERIC Document Reproduction Service No. ED378755)

Prearranged Options

When I feel:

1. _____

2. _____

3. _____

I will:

1. _____

2. _____

3. _____

I agree to return to the lesson within: _____

This agreement will be renegotiated on: _____

Signatures:

Student: _____

Classroom Teacher: _____

Special Education Teacher: _____

Parent: _____

_____: _____

_____: _____

5

Use Time Productively

Principle	Strategy
Use Time Productively	Establish Routines and Procedures
	Organize Physical Space
	Allocate Sufficient Time to Academic Activities

Chapter 5: Use Time Productively

Strategy:	**Establish Routines and Procedures**
Content Skills:	Arts; Fitness; Mathematics/Problem Solving/Calculating; Reading; Social Studies; Science
Learning Difference:	Study Skills; Receptive Language/Decoding (listening, reading); Processing Verbal Information; Attention; Cognition Low; Cognition Mixed; Memory Short-Term; Memory Long-Term; Fine Motor (handwriting, articulation, etc.); Processing Visual Information; Processing Verbal Information; Expressive Language/Encoding (speaking, writing, spelling)
Disability Category:	Specific Learning Disabilities; Serious Emotional Disturbance; Autism; Orthopedic or Other Health Impairments; Attention Deficit/Hyperactivity Disorder; Speech or Language Impairments; Traumatic Brain Injury; Multiple Disabilities; Mental Retardation; Hearing Impairments; Visual Impairments; Deafness/Blindness; Gifted and Talented

Tactic Title:	**Student Planners**
Problem:	Many students, particularly those with disabilities, have difficulty organizing themselves. They forget assignments, lose materials, and have no sense of timelines or due dates. For students who deal with several content areas and sets of requirements, learning to be better organized is essential.
Tactic:	Provide students with planners to enable them to record homework assignments, due dates, grades/scores, classroom rules, IEPs, etc. Provide places for students to record their daily assignments, as well as the grades they have received on these assignments. Grades received on quizzes and exams can also be recorded. Take a few minutes during each class to verify that every student has entered/recorded the appropriate information. Also, verify that students have obtained parent signatures.
Example:	My school doesn't provide planners for students, so I've made up my own version. At the beginning of each marking period, I provide the following: a list of Web sites so that students and parents can access school policies, procedures, and calendars (saves paper); the sections in the order in which I require students to organize their planners; and the way in which I expect each page (one for each day) to be organized. I also require my students to obtain parent signatures on a daily basis. So I'm pretty sure that parents know what is expected. Also, when students are required to keep track of their grades, they seem to try harder either to keep up their good work or improve it. Otherwise, graded papers get lost in notebooks, and students do not know how they are

doing. I encourage my students to treat their planner "like gold"; some are even using technology to "back up" the data.

Alicia T., teacher

Benefits: Student planners enable

- students to learn organizational skills;
- students to take greater personal responsibility in fulfilling assignments across teachers/content areas; and
- enhancement of collaboration among all the stakeholders: student, teachers, and parents.

Literature: Schneiderman, R. (with Werby, S.). (1996). *Homework improvement: A parent's guide to developing successful study habits in children before it's too late.* Tucson, AZ: Good Year Books.

Chapter 5: Use Time Productively

Strategy:	Organize Physical Space
Content Skills:	Arts; Fitness; Mathematics/Problem Solving/Calculating; Reading; Social Studies; Science; Writing
Learning Difference:	Cognition High; Cognition Low; Cognition Mixed; Attention; Processing Visual Information; Memory Short-Term; Memory Long-Term; Receptive Language/Decoding (listening, reading); Processing Verbal Information; Study Skills; Social Knowledge; Self-Control; Social Behaviors; Self-Confidence; Mobility; Hearing; Health; Seeing; Speaking/Talking; Fine Motor (handwriting, articulation, etc.); Gross Motor (running, walking, etc.); Expressive Language/Encoding (speaking, writing, spelling); Self-Care
Disability Category:	Attention Deficit/Hyperactivity Disorder; Orthopedic or Other Health Impairments; Autism; Second Language Learning Needs; Serious Emotional Disturbance; Specific Learning Disabilities; Speech or Language Impairments; Traumatic Brain Injury; Multiple Disabilities; Mental Retardation; Hearing Impairments; Gifted and Talented; Deafness/Blindness; Visual Impairments

Tactic Title:	Arranging the Physical Environment to Meet Everyone's Needs
Problem:	Different physical arrangements of classrooms facilitate different learning opportunities; they also convey messages to students as to what is expected of them. Traditional arrangements with desks in rows send the message that the teacher is the expert and all focus should be in his or her direction. Other secondary classrooms (such as science labs) may be "fixed" in different ways. This may be problematic for many learners *and* for teachers who seek different instructional options.
Tactic:	Consider your teaching responsibilities in the context of the instructional needs of each of your students. For example:

Teaching responsibilities: Will you be coteaching? Will you have paraprofessionals? Can your classroom be rearranged? If not, are there other places where you can teach?

Student instructional needs: Do all of your students have the same instructional goals/objectives? Who has an IEP that will involve specific instructional arrangements and/or accommodations?

Then, think about your teaching responsibilities and your students' instructional needs in the context of the classroom that you have. What are your options? How can you match your needs to those of your students? Be creative . . . take risks . . . talk to your colleagues (including the special education teachers) *and* your administrators/department chairs for ideas.

Example: I am fortunate to have a classroom where I can move things around a bit, although I have to be careful because some students cannot handle change as easily as others. I know that I have to start my classes in a structured way . . . students at their desks in rows or some other physical arrangement that gives them the message that I am in charge; they need to listen to me in order to know what to do. This is particularly important for students who are challenged in their learning. I also provide guidelines on the whiteboard and at the centers/tables where they will be working. After reviewing the expectations (both academic and behavior), they are much more able to deal with moving into other arrangements. I've tried it the other way . . . a recipe for disaster!

Santos R., teacher

Benefits: Appropriate flexible physical arrangements

- accommodate individual learning needs;
- provide teachers with more options in designing lessons; and
- minimize disruptions to learning and teaching.

Literature: Monberg, G. H., & Monberg, L. Z. (2006). Classrooms and teaching space. *School Planning & Management, 45*(2), 56–57.

Chapter 5: Use Time Productively

Strategy:	**Allocate Sufficient Time to Academic Activities**

Content Skills: Social Studies; Science; Writing

Learning Difference: Cognition Low; Receptive Language/Decoding (listening, reading); Expressive Language/Encoding (speaking, writing, spelling); Fine Motor (handwriting, articulation, etc.); Mobility; Self-Confidence

Disability Category: Mental Retardation; Visual Impairments; Traumatic Brain Injury; Specific Learning Disabilities; Speech or Language Impairments; Second Language Learning Needs; Serious Emotional Disturbance; Attention Deficit/Hyperactivity Disorder; Orthopedic or Other Health Impairments; Autism

Tactic Title:	**Using Assistive Technology (AT) to Enhance Writing**

Problem: Students with limited fine motor skills often find writing both physically difficult and extremely time consuming. Teachers also find it challenging to read the handwriting of these students.

Tactic: Use computers and word processing programs to increase your students' grammatical and spelling accuracy. Teach your students how to type and save their writing continually; their special education teacher or your AT specialist (if you're fortunate enough to have one) can help. Check students' IEPs to see whether AT is required. Then show them how to use spelling and grammar checks to edit and finalize their writing before printing the final version.

Example: I just love the fact that most of us have access to computers now; it has really helped so many of my students be able to exhibit their thinking in clear and "readable" ways. I know many struggle with spelling, handwriting, and grammar issues. However, I care much more that they understand the concepts that I'm trying to teach . . . that is my goal. We all take advantage of spelling and grammar checkers, calculators, etc., so why shouldn't we keep the focus on the content rather than the mechanics? I encourage my students to work in pairs as often as possible and to take advantage of every technological tool they can find to help them succeed.

Abby Y., teacher

Benefits: Students who have difficulty writing often find that using technology

- requires less fine motor control;
- decreases the amount of time they spend composing text; and
- decreases their frustration and increases their ability to express their ideas well.

Literature: Moffatt, C. W., Hanley-Maxwell, C., & Donnellan, A. M. (1995). Discrimination of emotion, affective perspective taking and empathy in individuals with mental retardation. *Education and Training in Mental Retardation and Developmental Disabilities, 30,* 76–84.

Shields, J., & Shealey, M. (1997). Educational computing gets powerful. *Technology and Learning, 18,* 20.

6

Establish Positive Environments

Principle	Strategy
Establish Positive Environments	Make the Classroom a Pleasant, Friendly Place
	Accept Individual Differences
	Establish Supportive, Cooperative Learning Environments
	Create a Nonthreatening Learning Environment

Chapter 6: Establish Positive Environments

Strategy:	**Make the Classroom a Pleasant, Friendly Place**
Content Skills:	Arts; Fitness; Mathematics/Problem Solving/Calculating; Reading; Social Studies; Science; Writing
Learning Difference:	Processing Verbal Information; Receptive Language/Decoding (listening, reading); Expressive Language/Encoding (speaking, writing, spelling); Processing Verbal Information; Processing Visual Information
Disability Category:	Second Language Learning Needs; Speech or Language Impairments

Tactic Title:	**Communicating With Students**
Problem:	Many students with language issues/disabilities have difficulty comprehending, speaking, and writing in a typical secondary classroom, where lectures, large-group discussions, and written assignments are the norm.
Tactic:	Create an atmosphere in your classroom that respects, honors, and welcomes diversity of all kinds: ability, disability, language, ethnicity, gender, culture, etc. Remember that language differences do not necessarily reflect intellectual levels. Make students feel welcome by incorporating elements of cultures (native languages and customs) into your lesson plans. When lecturing, provide study supplemental guides/outlines. During group discussions, note important points on the board or projector. Be supportive and encourage student participation. Accept accents to keep students actively participating and not withdrawing from the learning activities. For written assignments, let students work in carefully selected pairs. Finally, always provide supportive feedback about the activities or assignments they perform well.
Example:	I have several students in my class whose native language is Spanish; they have varied levels of skill with the English language. So I've used peers as learning partners who can restate, take notes, sometimes translate, and just make the Spanish speakers feel as though they have a "friend." And there's an added bonus. We're also finding that, as a class, we're all becoming a bit more fluent in a second language. ¡Mui bien! *Jack A., teacher*
Benefits:	Accommodating students with communication issues • enables students to feel more comfortable and welcome in your classroom; • provides opportunities for students to demonstrate their abilities in front of peers; and • provides more equitable learning experiences.

Literature: Webb-Johnson, G., Artiles, A. J., Trent, S. C., Jackson, C. W., & Velox, A. (1998). The status of research on multicultural education in teacher education and special education: Problems, pitfalls and promises. *Remedial and Special Education, 19*(1), 7–15.

Chapter 6: Establish Positive Environments

Strategy:	**Accept Individual Differences**

Content Skills:	Arts; Fitness; Mathematics/Problem Solving/Calculating; Reading; Social Studies; Science; Writing
Learning Difference:	Processing Visual Information; Memory Short-Term; Fine Motor (handwriting, articulation, etc.); Receptive Language/Decoding (listening, reading); Attention; Cognition High; Cognition Low; Mobility; Hearing; Health; Cognition Mixed; Memory Long-Term; Seeing; Speaking/Talking; Study Skills; Gross Motor (running, walking, etc.); Processing Verbal Information; Expressive Language/Encoding (speaking, writing, spelling); Social Knowledge; Self-Control; Social Behaviors; Self-Confidence; Self-Care
Disability Category:	Specific Learning Disabilities; Visual Impairments; Deafness/Blindness; Gifted and Talented; Traumatic Brain Injury; Multiple Disabilities; Mental Retardation; Hearing Impairments; Second Language Learning Needs; Serious Emotional Disturbance; Speech or Language Impairments; Autism; Orthopedic or Other Health Impairments; Attention Deficit/Hyperactivity Disorder

Tactic Title:	**Using Simulations to Increase Understanding and Sensitivity**

Problem:	Students who do not have a disability are often unaware and insensitive when it comes to understanding what it means to have a disability.
Tactic:	Simulations can facilitate a better understanding of the challenges and frustrations students with disabilities face. Develop a packet containing four worksheets (see Random Numbers Worksheets). The first three pages will appear to have the numbers 1–25 randomly scattered around the page, when, in fact, the first three pages should be identical in the strategic placement of the numbers. All even numbers are generally located in the top half of the page, and odd numbers in the bottom half. Using that format, each of the first three pages differs in initial appearance. For example, on page 1, the numeral 3 might be located on the lower left, and on page 2, on the lower right. On the fourth page, no strategic, planned format for placing numerals is used; odd and even numerals are placed at random.

1. Assign the first page. Tell the students to connect the numerals in sequence from 1 to 25 as quickly as they can. Time them for 60 seconds and have them record the number of numerals connected correctly.

2. Assign the second page with the same instructions. Time them for 60 seconds and have them record the number of numerals connected correctly.

3. Assign the third page with the same instructions. Time them for 60 seconds and have them record the number of numerals connected correctly.

4. Assign the fourth page with the same instructions. Time them for 60 seconds and have them record the number of numerals connected correctly. By the time students have completed the third page, students will have become familiar with the pattern and will be able to connect more numbers in less time. When they reach the fourth page, however, they become confused and, thus, score lower than before. Discuss their perceptions and feelings.

Example: I used simulations for years with my students; however, I take them on "disability walks." Each student is assigned to a group of five, each with a specified role that you determine. For example, I blindfold some students, tell others they do not understand English, tell another to pretend he or she has a broken arm, another that verbal communication is not an option, and one to be an observer/recorder. Then I send them off on a set of tasks: use the stairs, purchase a drink from a vending machine, ask someone for directions to a predetermined place, find a certain room in the school, etc. They have a limited time and must return to my classroom prior to the deadline. Then we "remove" the disability and share our observations and feelings. For homework, I ask them to reflect on the following topic: "What would be my life be like if the disability didn't go away?" I've found that this exercise is a wise use of class time as it sets the tone: this classroom is one where individual differences are welcomed and accepted.

Shannon H., teacher

Benefits: Simulations enable

- students to experience a different way of functioning, if only for a short time;
- students to reflect on what life might be like for someone with a disability or learning difference; and
- teachers to create a classroom that accepts differences as the norm.

Literature: Pearl, C. (2004). Laying the foundation for self-advocacy: Fourth graders with learning disabilities invite their peers into the resource room. *Teaching Exceptional Children, 36*(3), 44–49.

Random Numbers Worksheets

Random Numbers Worksheets

1.

1	25	11	17	23
9	3	23		
15			5	19
	21	13		7
	16			
6		22	14	
	4		18	24
		20	2	
12	24	8		10

2.

3	15	19	21	9
17				25
11	23	1	5	
		7	13	
2	18			
			12	6
8	14	4		
		10	22	
20	24		16	

3.

	15	21	13	
	3			17
7		9		
	25		1	5
19	11			23
	18		20	
12	4		10	2
14		8	6	22
	24		16	

4.

	24	17	10	7
2			23	18
	14	1		
8			20	4
				15
22	5			
11			9	13
	16	3		
19		25	21	
	6		12	

Chapter 6: Establish Positive Environments

Strategy:	**Establish Supportive, Cooperative Learning Environments**
Content Skills:	Arts; Fitness; Mathematics/Problem Solving/Calculating; Reading; Social Studies; Science; Writing
Learning Difference:	Social Knowledge; Social Behaviors; Self-Confidence; Self-Control
Disability Category:	Attention Deficit/Hyperactivity Disorder; Autism; Orthopedic or Other Health Impairments; Second Language Learning Needs; Specific Learning Disabilities; Serious Emotional Disturbance; Speech or Language Impairments; Traumatic Brain Injury; Multiple Disabilities; Hearing Impairments; Gifted and Talented; Deafness/Blindness; Visual Impairments

Tactic Title:	**Using Interactive Activities to Foster a Positive Classroom Atmosphere**
Problem:	Frequently, secondary students with disabilities have difficulty with social skills and peer relationships.
Tactic:	Divide the class into groups of four. Assign each a group a different story related to your content area or specialization—a story that involves self-control, anger management, and/or conflict resolution. Tell the groups to read the story together and then discuss the conclusion, perhaps using guided questions that you provide or the Alternate Conclusions Worksheet. Then give students time to create an alternative solution/conclusion. Finally, let students determine how they would like to tell the new story to their classmates—perhaps through some type of arts-related project, a written report, a PowerPoint presentation, etc.
Example:	Giving my students academic tasks that are embedded in "social" activities doesn't mean they aren't learning. In fact, giving them more control gets them much more involved. They take greater responsibility for their results and, therefore, learn more. That's important, of course; however, my hidden curriculum is also focused on including everyone and enabling everyone to be successful. I give them opportunities to practice their social skills and showcase their individual talents. In addition, I end up with a classroom where we all support and cooperate with one another; I have zero issues with behavior. It's a winner regardless of how you look at it. *Libby H., teacher*
Benefits:	Embedding academic lessons in interactive learning activities • enables students to practice their interpersonal/life skills; • fosters both academic and social learning; and • gives students a way to demonstrate their individual abilities, rather than highlight their disabilities.
Literature:	Dumas, M. C. (1998). The risk of social interaction: Problems among adolescents with ADHD. *Education and Treatment of Children, 21,* 447–460.

Alternate Conclusions Worksheet

Directions: Give this worksheet to groups to use as a guide during their discussions. The back of the worksheet can be used to illustrate alternative endings. Encourage students to be creative and innovative in their thinking.

Group Member: **Role:**

_____   _____

_____   _____

_____   _____

_____   _____

_____   _____

_____   _____

Story Title:_____

Ideas for Alternate Conclusions:

1. _____

2. _____

3. _____

4. _____

5. _____

6. _____

Circle # of final selection.

Describe how your group made its final selection:

Chapter 6: Establish Positive Environments

Strategy:	**Create a Nonthreatening Learning Environment**
Content Skills:	Arts; Fitness; Mathematics/Problem Solving/Calculating; Reading; Social Studies; Science; Writing
Learning Difference:	Attention; Study Skills
Disability Category:	Specific Learning Disabilities; Visual Impairments; Deafness/Blindness; Gifted and Talented; Traumatic Brain Injury; Multiple Disabilities; Mental Retardation; Hearing Impairments; Second Language Learning Needs; Serious Emotional Disturbance; Speech or Language Impairments; Autism; Orthopedic or Other Health Impairments; Attention Deficit/Hyperactivity Disorder

Tactic Title:	**Staying Organized**
Problem:	Teachers often find that students with disabilities struggle with organization.
Tactic:	To help students organize their academic tasks, keep daily routines and schedules consistent and prominently displayed. Teach students to estimate the time they might need to complete tasks and use a calendar or homework planner. Teach students to make lists, break large projects into smaller parts, and plan for future assignments. Give time in class to begin homework. Finally, establish a cooperative homework team between the student with a disability and another student who tends to be well organized and dependable. Partners can call each other when homework is due and work together in and out of class to complete assignments.
Benefits:	I think that teaching organizational skills is equally, if not more, important than teaching subject area content. It is a basic life skill and is applicable across all of a student's classes. *Eloy R., teacher*
Benefits:	Using peers as partners • enables students who are disorganized to submit assignments on time; • creates a support network for students with disabilities; and • fosters a collaborative supportive classroom.
Literature:	Stormont-Spurgin, M. (1997). I lost my homework: Strategies for improving organization in students with ADHD. *Intervention in School and Clinic, 32,* 270–274.

PART III

Delivering Instruction

Teaching is systematic presentation of content. Effective teachers present information in carefully monitored lessons, which they adjust to meet the needs of their students. In this part of our resource, we describe evidence-based strategies for each principle of delivering instruction.

Component	Principle	Strategy
Delivering Instruction (Part III)	Present Information (Chapter 7)	*Presenting Content* Gain and Maintain Attention Review Prior Skills or Lessons Provide Organized, Relevant Lessons
		Motivating Students Show Enthusiasm and Interest Use Rewards Effectively Consider Level and Student Interest
		Teaching Thinking Skills Model Thinking Skills Teach Fact-Finding Skills Teach Divergent Thinking Teach Learning Strategies
		Providing Relevant Practice Develop Automaticity Vary Opportunities for Practice Vary Methods of Practice Monitor Amount of Work Assigned
	Monitor Presentations (Chapter 8)	*Providing Feedback* Give Immediate, Frequent, Explicit Feedback Provide Specific Praise and Encouragement

(Continued)

(Continued)

	Model Correct Performance
	Provide Prompts and Cues
	Check Student Understanding
	Keeping Students Actively Involved
	Monitor Performance Regularly
	Monitor Performance During Practice
	Use Peers to Improve Instruction
	Provide Opportunities for Success
	Limit Opportunities for Failure
	Monitor Engagement Rates
Adjust Presentations (Chapter 9)	Adapt Lessons to Meet Student Needs
	Provide Varied Instructional Options
	Alter Pace

Delivering Instruction Works: A Case Study

As a high school history teacher for over 20 years, I pride myself on delivering instruction in a variety of ways to my students. I have found that in my own learning, I appreciate varied methods, and many students have commented in the past about how it was easier to pay attention when the same method of delivering instruction was not the same for each lesson. I frequently have the students work in pairs and groups and, at times, individually. I use centers in my classroom and have found that a rolling cart with sliding drawers is very effective. I also create games or have my students create games centered on a topic or concept that we are learning about in history. (Related tactic is located in Chapter 9: Adjust Presentations under Strategy: Provide Varied Instructional Options.)

7

Present Information

Component	Principle	Strategy
Delivering Instruction	Present Information	*Presenting Content* Gain and Maintain Attention Review Prior Skills or Lessons Provide Organized, Relevant Lessons *Motivating Students* Show Enthusiasm and Interest Use Rewards Effectively Consider Level and Student Interest *Teaching Thinking Skills* Model Thinking Skills Teach Fact-Finding Skills Teach Divergent Thinking Teach Learning Strategies *Providing Relevant Practice* Develop Automaticity Vary Opportunities for Practice Vary Methods of Practice Monitor Amount of Work Assigned

Chapter 7: Present Information

Strategy:	Gain and Maintain Attention

Content Skills:	Arts; Fitness; Mathematics/Problem Solving/Calculating; Reading; Social Studies; Science; Writing
Learning Difference:	Attention; Processing Verbal Information
Disability Category:	Specific Learning Disabilities; Attention Deficit/Hyperactivity Disorder; Serious Emotional Disturbance; Mental Retardation; Multiple Disabilities

Tactic Title:	Using Eye Contact as a Cue for Students With Attention Issues

Problem:	Some students find that focusing on a specific task and maintaining their attention over time are especially challenging. Teachers can provide a variety of visual, verbal, and nonverbal cues to refocus attention and promote on-task behavior.
Tactic:	In activities where the entire class is involved (such as when the teacher gives directions), nonverbal, visual cues can be the least invasive intervention. Cues that have been agreed upon previously are the most effective and unobtrusive. First, it is essential to gain the attention of each student. Simply wait or stop talking yourself. When it is evident that every student is attending, then begin/continue. Repeat whenever necessary. If an individual student's attention is wandering provide the visual cue to the student that she or he needs to refocus. You could make eye contact with the student and point with the index and middle fingers first at the student's eyes, then back at your own eyes. In effect, you are giving a nonverbal signal to the student that "you need to pay attention to me now," without the embarrassment or disruption of a verbal intervention in front of the class. (See the Visual Cues list that follows.)
Example:	Nonverbal cues are an effective strategy when working with any group of students, not just those with specific attention issues. All students have a day now and then when school and my class, in particular, are not on their "agenda." Unobtrusive cues allow me to continue teaching. However, I'm always aware of two factors: (1) the reason for their inattention may be directly related to their disability—thus, I try to keep the situation informal and positive and (2) the content may be too difficult, easy, uninteresting, or misunderstood—that's my fault, and I try to adjust as quickly as possible.

Delia N., teacher

Benefits: Nonverbal visual cues are unobtrusive yet powerful ways to refocus the attention of individual students without disrupting instruction or potentially embarrassing them in front of their classmates. Specifically, they

- maintain the focus on instruction and learning;
- teach students to gain control of their own behavior; and
- can be individualized to minimize student embarrassment.

Literature: Barkley, P. (1993). Eight principles to guide ADHD children. *The ADHD Report, 1*(2), 1–4.

Visual Cues

1. Touch your mouth.

2. Touch your eyes.

3. Pull your earlobe.

4. Use eye-to-eye contact.

5. Cross your arms.

6. Put your hand on your hip.

7. Tilt your head.

8. Move your head in a specified direction.

9. Look puzzled.

10. Make a predetermine noise (for example, whistle, sigh, moan, etc.).

11. Sing.

12. Clear your throat.

13. Look up at the ceiling.

14. Turn around in a circle.

15. Point to a picture on chalk/dry erase board or elsewhere in the classroom.

16. Move closer to student.

17. Stand next to student.

18. Touch student's desk/table.

19. Put agreed-upon object on student's desk to redirect attention.

20. Create your own . . .

Chapter 7: Present Information

Strategy:	**Review Prior Skills or Lessons**
Content Skills:	Arts; Fitness; Mathematics/Problem Solving/Calculating; Reading; Social Studies; Science; Writing
Learning Difference:	Speaking/Talking; Attention; Processing Visual Information; Memory Short-Term; Receptive Language/Decoding (listening, reading); Self-Confidence; Cognition Low; Hearing; Cognition Mixed; Memory Long-Term; Seeing; Study Skills; Processing Verbal Information; Expressive Language/Encoding (speaking, writing, spelling)
Disability Category:	Visual Impairments; Deafness/Blindness; Gifted and Talented; Hearing Impairments; Mental Retardation; Multiple Disabilities; Traumatic Brain Injury; Second Language Learning Needs; Serious Emotional Disturbance; Specific Learning Disabilities; Speech or Language Impairments; Attention Deficit/Hyperactivity Disorder; Orthopedic or Other Health Impairments; Autism

Tactic Title:	**Modification of Teaching Style for Students With ADHD**
Problem:	It is often frustrating and discouraging when some students with special needs, such as ADHD, are not able to pay attention to instruction and lecture material.
Tactic:	This tactic is perfect for reviewing previously discussed material for a test or final examination. First, divide the class into two groups with diverse learners. Have each group select its team name. Establish an appropriate and motivating reward for the winning team, as well as a consolation prize for the team that loses. Review the rules that are used for the competition: no talking out, use the signal, remain in seat, etc. Then have one representative from the first group stand. Pose a question regarding previously studied material to his or her team. Team members use an appropriate pre-arranged signal (thumbs-up, finger on head, arms folded, etc.) to indicate that they have a response. Select one student to respond for his or her team. After the response is given, ask the student who is standing whether the response was correct or incorrect. If he or she says that the answer was correct (and it was), that team earns a point; if the standing student identifies a correct answer as being incorrect *or* an incorrect answer as being correct, the opposing team earns a point. Next, select a member of the other team and repeat the process with a new question. The team with the most points at the end wins!
Example:	I love integrating games and contests into learning activities because my students are so involved in the challenge. Structuring a game/contest in this way makes everyone in the group responsible for teammates and fosters cooperative and supportive behaviors. I've also found

that preparing for tests this way has had a positive effect on their grades. I also have the flexibility to "control" the questions and adjust the format and content according to the student who is standing *and* the team member I select. I can see its use across content areas.

Nya P., teacher

Benefits: Using cooperative learning activities in game formats

- encourages cooperation among all students;
- increases the ability of students to focus and pay attention; and
- is motivating, effective, and fun.

Literature: Griffin, L. L., & Butler, J. I. (Eds.) (2005). *Teaching games for understanding: Theory, research, and practice.* Champaign, IL: Human Kinetics.

Chapter 7: Present Information

Strategy:	**Provide Organized, Relevant Lessons**
Content Skills:	Arts; Fitness; Mathematics/Problem Solving/Calculating; Reading; Social Studies; Science; Writing
Learning Difference:	Processing Visual Information; Cognition Mixed; Processing Verbal Information; Receptive Language/Decoding (listening, reading); Expressive Language/Encoding (speaking, writing, spelling)
Disability Category:	Attention Deficit/Hyperactivity Disorder; Second Language Learning Needs; Serious Emotional Disturbance; Specific Learning Disabilities; Speech or Language Impairments; Mental Retardation; Traumatic Brain Injury

Tactic Title:	**Using Visual Aids, Realia, and Manipulatives to Enhance Student Learning**
Problem:	Regardless of student age or grade level, disability/ability, or content area, many students need to see/touch/manipulate the underpinning of the concepts you are teaching.
Tactic:	When introducing new material, provide visual aids (realia, manipulatives, etc.). For example, in science, when describing the parts of flowers and their importance in the fertilization process, provide real plants with diagrams for students to observe and explore. In mathematics, provide real models of geometric or algebraic concepts you are introducing. In English, art, physical education, music, and other content areas, use video and audio to show students what you are expecting them to learn and understand. Provide specific guidelines as to what they must be looking for, possibly a handout with an example and with key components labeled. Demonstrate how they might use one component of the visual aids/realia/manipulatives and discuss why it is relevant to their assignment. Next, allow the students to find their own unique example(s) using the guidelines that you provided. Give them a specified time to complete this task. Then ask individual students to present their examples to the class. Ask them to explain why they chose that example (including the qualities it has that fit the given guidelines) and where they found/observed/experienced it in using the visual aids/realia/manipulatives that you provided.
Example:	Regardless of the age and/or grade level or ability of my students, realia is where I begin. If they don't connect with what I'm trying to teach, it's over. So, YouTube, guest speakers, manipulatives, videos, podcasts . . . you name it. . . . If it's credible—and I mean credible (a truly trusted source)—I am prepared to use it, *and* I am not above designing my own materials . . . bringing in objects and examples that I just dream up, can find, or have on hand. If I believe they will help engage my students

in learning the concept, I'm there. I'm not going to tell you my content/ subject area, because I want you to be thinking about your own and what you can use to make learning real for your students.

Gabriel R., teacher

Benefits: Visual aids can

- enable students to become actively involved in their own learning;
- provide a focal point/reference for students as they proceed through subsequent related lessons; and
- improve students learning as they move through the stages of learning new concepts: acquisition, proficiency, maintenance, and generalization.

Literature: Mulcahy, C. A. (2008). The effects of a contextualized instructional package on the area and perimeter performance of secondary students with emotional and behavioral disabilities (Doctoral dissertation, University of Maryland, 2007). *Dissertation Abstracts International, 68*, 8-A.

Chapter 7: Present Information

Strategy:	Show Enthusiasm and Interest

Content Skills:	Mathematics/Problem Solving/Calculating

Learning Difference: Expressive Language/Encoding (speaking, writing, spelling); Attention; Cognition Mixed; Processing Visual Information; Cognition High; Cognition Low; Mobility; Hearing; Health; Memory Short-Term; Memory Long-Term; Seeing; Speaking/Talking; Study Skills; Processing Verbal Information; Receptive Language/Decoding (listening, reading); Self-Control

Disability Category: Specific Learning Disabilities; Visual Impairments; Deafness/Blindness; Gifted and Talented; Hearing Impairments; Mental Retardation; Multiple Disabilities; Traumatic Brain Injury; Second Language Learning Needs; Serious Emotional Disturbance; Speech or Language Impairments; Attention Deficit/Hyperactivity Disorder; Orthopedic or Other Health Impairments; Autism

Tactic Title:	Mathematics in Daily Life

Problem: Students have difficulty in mathematics because of their disability (reading, memory, visual processing, etc.) or simply because they do not see its relevance to their lives.

Tactic: First, decide on an activity that you know the student will use in the future—for example, learning to manage a budget. You could create an "economy" within your classroom, where students are "paid" for the number of hours they are in school and/or the amount and quality of the work they produce. Then they could develop a financial plan that would list their expenses (rent, utilities, insurance, food, medical, entertainment, etc.). Based on this plan, you can teach them how to manage a checking account, follow the stock market, etc. while integrating your required curriculum into the activities. This activity continues through the whole year but expands every couple of months. For example, they might have to calculate the tax that is taken out of their check or decide which kind of car insurance to buy.

Example: This tactic gives students the opportunity to review and apply concepts like percentages, multiplication, and other mathematical functions; having these basic skills is essential for successful learning of higher thinking concepts. It also answers the question: "Why do I have to learn this?" by making the curriculum real. It certainly is appropriate for the secondary level because so many students just don't have the foundational skills they will need. Finally, I really enjoy teaching this way . . . makes classes so much more interesting and fun!

Randi A., teacher

Benefits: Using a life skills curriculum in content areas

- helps students understand the importance and relevance of the subject;
- is effective across content areas, disability categories, and learning differences; and
- makes learning and teaching fun.

Literature: Saarimaki, P. (1995). Math in your world. *National Council of Teachers, 9,* 565–569.

Chapter 7: Present Information

Strategy:	Use Rewards Effectively

Content Skills:	Arts; Fitness; Mathematics/Problem Solving/Calculating; Reading; Social Studies; Science; Writing

Learning Difference:	Attention; Study skills; Cognition High; Cognition Low; Mobility; Hearing; Seeing; Memory Long-Term; Memory Short-Term; Cognition Mixed; Health; Speaking/Talking; Fine Motor (handwriting, articulation, etc.); Gross Motor (running, walking, etc.); Processing Visual Information; Self-Control; Social Knowledge; Expressive Language/ Encoding (speaking, writing, spelling); Receptive Language/Decoding (listening, reading); Processing Verbal Information; Social Behaviors; Self-Confidence; Self-Care

Disability Category:	Attention Deficit/Hyperactivity Disorder; Autism; Orthopedic or Other Health Impairments; Speech or Language Impairments; Second Language Learning Needs; Serious Emotional Disturbance; Specific Learning Disabilities; Hearing Impairments; Mental Retardation; Multiple Disabilities; Traumatic Brain Injury; Gifted and Talented; Deafness/Blindness; Visual Impairments; Attention Deficit Disorder

Tactic Title:	Homework Charts

Problem:	Some students need extra assistance to complete long-term homework assignments, such as reports or research projects. A system that provides an extra incentive for completion is often needed.
Tactic:	After outlining and discussing the assignment, make sure the student understands what he or she is required to do and enters the assignment in his or her homework/assignment planner (see the Homework Reminder). Provide a reminder or check sheet that the student can use while working through the assignment. Then review the check sheet with the student periodically and award points for reaching intermediate benchmarks. Record completed assignments on a homework chart. When a predetermined number of assignments has been completed, the student earns extra credit toward the grade for the marking period.
Example:	I make sure that the homework chart is stapled into the student's planner and is signed by parents nightly. I also make a copy for myself in case the planner is "misplaced." I've found that the rate of assignment completion has improved greatly during the last couple of months and students can actually "see" their progress. I just use a simple chart with the assignment title and due date on the left and a tally mark in the "On Time" or "Not on Time" columns on the right. We keep a running total with percentages at the bottom. Keeps it clear and simple.

Andy P., teacher

Benefits: Homework charts

- are a great reinforcer for students;
- provide an accessible, visible record of their achievements and needs over time; and
- improve self-esteem, confidence, and responsibility.

Literature: Bryan, T., & Sullivan-Burstein, K. (1998). From behavior to constructivism in teacher education. *Remedial and Special Education Journal, 19,* 263–275.

Homework Reminder

Name:_____

Title of Assignment: _____   Due Date:_____

Today is: _____   I have _____ weeks/days to complete this assignment.

I need to:

1. _____ by _____

2. _____ by _____

3. _____ by _____

4. _____ by _____

5. _____ by _____

6. _____ by _____

7. _____ by _____

8. _____ by _____

Resources needed:

Strategies I will use:

Dates of teacher conferences:

Chapter 7: Present Information

Strategy:	**Consider Level and Student Interest**

Content Skills: Writing; Science; Social Studies; Reading

Learning Difference: Social Knowledge; Study Skills; Expressive Language/Encoding (speaking, writing, spelling); Self-Confidence

Disability Category: Specific Learning Disabilities; Visual Impairments; Serious Emotional Disturbance; Speech or Language Impairments; Second Language Learning Needs; Mental Retardation; Attention Deficit/Hyperactivity Disorder; Autism

Tactic Title:	**Using Computers to Improve Reading**

Problem: Teachers and educators often find that, for many students with special needs, printed books can be more of a barrier than a pathway to learning.

Tactic: First, identify students with special needs in your classroom and review their individual learning styles and reading levels (noted on their IEPs). Next, in collaboration with your special education teacher, provide appropriate software that "reads" text for students at their individual performance levels. Ensure that students understand the assignment, know how to operate the computer and software, and are able to function individually or with a peer at the computer. Finally, ensure that the assignment provides an opportunity for students to contribute at their levels of competency.

Example: I can remember what it was like to teach my subject area without computers and how my students with reading disabilities used to struggle. Now, with textbooks that include glossaries for vocabulary development; related Internet sources; and text with headers and gloss notes on the side, lots of pictures, learning objectives, and summary questions with suggested activities, students have so many pathways to understanding the material. Adding technology to the mix has given my students with reading disabilities the extra support they need, and we can use the supplemental resources that fit with individual student interests. Now when Sarah, the special education teacher, and I coteach, we really coteach and work with all the students together.

Ben R., teacher

Benefits: Computers and multimedia technologies

- motivate learning;
- aid in social interaction
- build self-esteem; and
- provide students with disabilities additional ways of communicating.

Literature: Holzberg, C. S. (1995). Beyond the printed book. *Technology and Learning, 15,* 22–23.

Chapter 7: Present Information

Strategy:	Model Thinking Skills
Content Skills:	Social Studies; Science; Writing
Learning Difference:	Expressive Language/Encoding (speaking, writing, spelling); Attention; Cognition Low; Memory Short-Term; Memory Long-Term; Cognition Mixed; Processing Visual Information; Processing Verbal Information; Receptive Language/Decoding (listening, reading)
Disability Category:	Specific Learning Disabilities; Mental Retardation; Attention Deficit/ Hyperactivity Disorder; Autism; Second Language Learning Needs; Serious Emotional Disturbance; Speech or Language Impairments

Tactic Title:	Forming a Comprehensible Composition
Problem:	Many students with disabilities are challenged to produce comprehensible, meaningful compositions; in some cases, they simply lack the confidence needed to do so.
Tactic:	First, divide students into medium-sized groups of five or six. A topic that you have selected and posted will be the basis for the compositions that they will write. Topics might include the following: What I do when . . . , How I find . . . , I like the writing of . . . . Topics may be more structured depending on the focus of your instruction/lesson/content area, such as Shakespeare's writing . . . . Ask each group to brainstorm ideas based on the topic. One idea often sparks another that one student alone might not have thought of. Have students develop subtopics and then topic sentences, as well as a list of descriptive words and phrases that could accompany the subtopics. Then have each group share their outlines, topic sentences, and descriptive words/phrases with the whole class, as well as a rationale/ defense as to why they think their presentation is the best.

The next step would be to have students begin to write their compositions. You can decide whether this should be an individual, pair, or small-group assignment. You also choose to vary the required number of paragraphs according to student abilities/needs, vary the time frame, and/or set different criteria for grading compositions.

At some point, provide time for reviewing and editing draft submissions, revising, and resubmitting the final product. Again, you can structure any of these steps in various ways according to student needs/abilities. You might decide to re-form the groups for a peer-editing session, engage everyone in a review of their work thus far, etc. The important component is giving students the opportunity to rethink and revise their work. Revision of the composition—paragraph by paragraph or in its entirety—is a repeating process until compositions are completed.

The final step is "publication." All compositions will be shared in some format, which you and/or your students determine.

Example: I've found it so important to find ways to let everyone complete the "same" assignment but sometimes in very different ways. Sometimes, I even break it down to the level of sentences, rather than paragraphs. Using peers in this way frees me to monitor their progress and provide individual assistance. I also like to give my students time to use their journals to reflect on how the process/assignment worked or did not work for them. Reading their journals gives me one more way to assess their abilities and instructional needs. I never, ever grade journals. That would stifle their feeling free to write what they honestly think and feel.

Ann R., teacher

Benefits: Using peers to model thinking skills

- builds confidence while teaching the process for developing a comprehensible essay;
- enables students to collaborate with peers in a nonthreatening way;
- encourages students to take responsibility for one another's learning; and
- allows students actually to "see" examples of acceptable compositions.

Literature: Graham, S., Schwartz, S., & MacArthur, C. (1993). Knowledge of writing and the composing process, attitude toward writing, and self-efficiency for students with and without learning disabilities. *Journal of Learning Disabilities, 26,* 237–249.

Chapter 7: Present Information

Strategy:	Teach Fact-Finding Skills
Content Skills:	Social Studies; Science; Writing
Learning Difference:	Speaking/Talking; Cognition Mixed; Attention; Processing Visual Information; Study Skills; Receptive Language/Decoding (listening, reading); Expressive Language/Encoding (speaking, writing, spelling); Fine Motor (handwriting, articulation, etc.); Processing Verbal Information; Self-Confidence; Processing Verbal Information
Disability Category:	Specific Learning Disabilities; Visual Impairments; Deafness/Blindness; Hearing Impairments; Mental Retardation; Multiple Disabilities; Traumatic Brain Injury; Gifted and Talented; Second Language Learning Needs; Serious Emotional Disturbance; Speech or Language Impairments; Attention Deficit/Hyperactivity Disorder; Orthopedic or Other Health Impairments; Autism

Tactic Title:	Teaching Fact-Finding Skills Step by Step
Problem:	Using information (facts) to provide the foundation for and inclusion in reports is frequently challenging for students who lack experience or ability in searching effectively for specific information.
Tactic:	The first step is to teach students how to recognize information when they see it. Use your text(s) and practice finding the answers together to specific questions (which you provide). Teach them how to note/record the specific page number, paragraph/sentence number, and the exact word(s) that answer(s) the question.
	Another exercise would be to give students just a subject/topic/question and ask them to find it wherever it is mentioned in their text. This requires them to use table of contents and indexes.
	Then collaborate with your school librarian in a session or two that would demonstrate the resources available to students there. Be sure to talk about ways to finding credible resources on the Internet that have reliable and trustworthy information.
	Finally, assign a topic to your students that requires them to use their fact-finding skills.
Example:	When I am teaching fact-finding skills, I typically divide the class into teams of students with diverse learning abilities/needs to make this assignment a competition. The goal is to find the most credible and accurate facts related to the question/topic that I assign. We spend an entire class session reviewing each team's findings *and* the resources they used—*and* how they

found them. After this, I can begin to assign research projects because they know where to look for excellent information.

Claudia G., teacher

Benefits:

Taking the time to teach fact-finding skills in a step-by-step way

- teaches students many strategies for finding information;
- provides options for students of varying abilities and needs; and
- ultimately improves the quality of student work and saves teacher time.

Literature:

Drueke, J., & Streckfuss, R. (1996). Some first steps in teaching a strategy for fact finding. *Journalism and Mass Communication Educator, 51*(2), 5–79.

Chapter 7: Present Information

Strategy:	**Teach Divergent Thinking**
Content Skills:	Science
Learning Difference:	Speaking/Talking; Cognition Mixed; Attention; Processing Visual Information; Study Skills; Receptive Language/Decoding (listening, reading); Expressive Language/Encoding (speaking, writing, spelling); Fine Motor (handwriting, articulation, etc.); Processing Verbal Information; Self-Confidence; Processing Verbal Information
Disability Category:	Specific Learning Disabilities; Visual Impairments; Deafness/Blindness; Hearing Impairments; Mental Retardation; Multiple Disabilities; Traumatic Brain Injury; Gifted and Talented; Second Language Learning Needs; Serious Emotional Disturbance; Speech or Language Impairments; Attention Deficit/Hyperactivity Disorder; Orthopedic or Other Health Impairments; Autism

Tactic Title:	**Using Hands-On, Student-Designed Experiments and Projects**
Problem:	Many students believe that the freedom to do things in more than one way is not an option. However, thinking creatively is really a basic life skill.
Tactic:	When students are given the option of thinking differently and still succeeding, the results can be astounding—especially when students with diverse learning needs are included. For example, in an experiment on sedimentary and igneous rocks, first ask students to choose two other students to work with. Retain the option to rearrange the groups based on student abilities/needs and your knowledge of the "big classroom picture." Your goal is to create groups that are diverse yet functional. Grouping all the students with disabilities in one group is *not* an option.
	Next, demonstrate how to layer bread in a pattern and wrap the stack in wax paper. You might have students take a picture of the way their stack looks at this point. Next, students select three slices of two different colored breads—for instance, one rye, two white, etc.—and layer each on top of another. Together with your students, brainstorm a list of ideas as to how their stack might look if pressure was applied from the top. Pressure might be a hand, an iron, a brick, a jackhammer, a dictionary, etc.
	Then students within each group choose one "stomper" to place the wrapped bread on the floor and step on it until it is relatively flat. Another student is chosen to unwrap the bread and cut it in half to examine the layers of color and the flatness of the bread. Take a second photograph for comparison.

Then conduct a discussion about the way time, weight, and density affect the formation of rock with students presenting their before/after comparisons. If there is time, you could take one stack of already flattened bread and stomp on it while a student stomps on another. Together, the class can evaluate how a difference in weight can result in a remarkable difference in rock formations. From this point, students can develop their own projects on rocks. They can choose certain properties to examine (color, uses, origin, interesting facts), and make mobiles to display their findings. Students choose which facts to include and use appropriate colors to identify the rocks on the mobile (e.g., amethyst = purple).

Finally, take time to review their predictions and compare them with the observations of the actual results.

Example: I'm always looking for "real" ways to teach my students to think in different ways, and this tactic provides so many ideas. It helps them relate everyday materials to the study of my subject area—mathematics. As a follow-up activity, I would have my students write in their journals . . . reflecting on whether or how their original ideas helped them understand the results and/or their own learning.

Sylvia R., teacher

Benefits: Teaching students that their own creative ideas have value

- involves students directly in their learning;
- applies across content/subject areas; and
- fosters a community of learners where all sorts of creative possibilities are welcomed and valued.

Literature: Rose, T. D. (1999). Middle school teachers: Using individualized instruction strategies. *Intervention in School and Clinic, 34*(3), 137–142.

Chapter 7: Present Information

Strategy:	Teach Learning Strategies

Content Skills:	Social Studies; Science; Mathematics/Problem Solving/Calculating; Reading
Learning Difference:	Cognition High; Cognition Low; Cognition Mixed; Attention; Processing Visual Information; Study Skills; Social Knowledge; Memory Short-Term; Memory Long-Term; Receptive Language/Decoding (listening, reading); Expressive Language/Encoding (speaking, writing, spelling); Processing Verbal Information; Self-Confidence; Processing Verbal Information; Hearing; Health; Speaking/Talking; Fine Motor (hand-writing, articulation, etc.)
Disability Category:	Specific Learning Disabilities; Attention Deficit/Hyperactivity Disorder; Gifted and Talented; Traumatic Brain Injury; Second Language Learning Needs; Serious Emotional Disturbance; Orthopedic or Other Health Impairments; Autism; Speech or Language Impairments; Mental Retardation

Tactic Title:	Empowering Students to Facilitate Their Own Learning

Problem:	Many students have difficulty focusing on relevant information in reading material.
Tactic:	Highlighters are a wonderful support for students, and they love using them! Teach them about the concept of highlighting first, because students tend to highlight everything, but after observing modeling and hearing an explanation of the purpose of highlighting, they understand. Then, when reading aloud to students as they follow along with their own copy of the text, encourage them to highlight the information they think is important. Discuss the portions of the text that various students have highlighted and why they thought those portions were important. Explore ways in which the highlighting might need to be edited (cut/expanded).
Example:	I highlight, you highlight, we all highlight. The trick is in knowing how to highlight correctly *or* how to take those highlights and determine the essential points contained within them. I admit: I am an overhighlighter . . . *Guilty!* However, I will not stop highlighting, because it does help me focus on what's important and then winnow it down. I teach my students with an overhighlighting disability like mine how *I* deal with this problem . . . it's simple. Review the material that has been highlighted, take a different color highlighter, and rehighlight the essential points contained within the original highlights. . . . Repeat as needed and then make a list of the final essential points. Trust me, it works in my content area . . . should also work in others.

Betsy Y., teacher

Benefits: When students use highlighting as a strategy in their learning, students learn to:

- identify important information;
- learn ways to preplan before writing and researching; and
- take greater confidence in their own ability to identify essential information.

Literature: Fowler, R. L. (1974). Effectiveness of highlighting for retention of text material. *Journal of Applied Psychology, 59,* 358–364.

Chapter 7: Present Information

Strategy:	**Develop Automaticity**

Content Skills:	Arts; Fitness; Mathematics/Problem Solving/Calculating; Reading; Social Studies; Science; Writing
Learning Difference:	Attention; Study Skills; Processing Verbal Information; Cognition High; Cognition Low; Mobility; Hearing; Health; Cognition Mixed; Memory Short-Term; Memory Long-Term; Seeing; Speaking/Talking; Fine Motor (handwriting, articulation, etc.); Gross Motor (running, walking, etc.); Processing Visual Information; Processing Verbal Information; Receptive Language/Decoding (listening, reading); Expressive Language/Encoding (speaking, writing, spelling); Social Knowledge; Self-Control; Social Behaviors; Self-Confidence; Self-Care
Disability Category:	Attention Deficit/Hyperactivity Disorder; Visual Impairments; Deafness/Blindness; Gifted and Talented; Hearing Impairments; Mental Retardation; Multiple Disabilities; Traumatic Brain Injury; Second Language Learning Needs; Serious Emotional Disturbance; Specific Learning Disabilities; Speech or Language Impairments; Orthopedic or Other Health Impairments; Autism

Tactic Title:	**Moving From Just "Doing" to "Doing Well"**

Problem:	Students are often able to learn a concept or skill and find the correct answer in a constant context, if given enough time. However, under real circumstances/different contexts that require the ability to apply what they know, students frequently fail. Making this transition in their learning is especially important for students with diverse learning needs.
Tactic:	In learning new concepts, students need to be guided by their teachers through the four stages of learning: acquisition, automaticity/proficiency, maintenance, and generalization (see the following figure). When teaching/reteaching skills so that students can move from the acquisition stage of learning (up to 80 percent accurate yet needing too much time, or really fast in finishing with too many errors) to the automatic/proficient stage, include time in your lesson plans for students to practice their rudimentary skills. Give them at least 10–15 minutes per period to practice to achieve 80–90 percent accuracy. Supplement with additional homework assignments to give them opportunities to refine their accuracy and speed. Chart in-class and homework rates and include the data in student portfolios.
Example:	The way I learned to understand the importance of the acquisition stage of learning or automaticity was to think of one of my students learning how to drive. He or she knew the basics: how to turn the key, back up,

move the gear shift into "drive" or "reverse," and use the brake pedal to stop. OK . . . good, but not good enough. If I'm at a crossroads waiting for my red light to turn green, I do not want to move into the intersection thinking that the drivers to my right or left are really great at using the brake pedal, but not always in time . . . or that they see the red light in time but may step on the gas pedal instead of the brake. Not sufficient. Needless to say, I give my students time to practice and improve both their accuracy and speed. Time well spent; they improve in both ways, and we can then move on to integrating (maintaining) and generalizing these skills into subsequent lessons.

Abby T., teacher

Benefits: Integrating time into class and homework assignments

- provides the time that students need to refine and expand their basic acquisition-level skills;
- benefits all students by ensuring that they are practicing the skills they have already attained (not errors); and
- enables teachers to move more quickly through their curriculum.

Literature: Bloom, B. S. (1986). Automaticity: The hands and feet of genius. *Educational Leadership, 43*(5), 70–77.

Instructional Planning and Learning Phases

	Acquisition	Proficiency	Maintenance	Generalization
Goal	To increase probability of correct responses	To increase frequency of correct responses / To develop high rates of correct responses	To maintain high frequencies and rates of correct responses over time	To maintain high frequencies and rates of correct responses over time and across situations
Learner Characteristics	Skill Introduction / Naive / Unskilled / Low accuracy/low speed	Skill Mastery / High accuracy and speed	Independence / High accuracy and speed	Application / High accuracy and speed
Instructional Characteristics	Intense teacher-student interaction	Fading teacher-student interaction	Fading teacher-student interaction	Fading teacher-student interaction
Instruction	Teacher: Model, Demonstrate, Explain, Examples/ nonexamples, Prompt, Guide, Cue, Feedback (corrective/supportive) — Student: Imitate, Respond	Teacher: Fading, Intermittent reminders — Student: Drill, Fast pace, Practice, massed, guided to independence	Teacher: Fade cues, Detail, Prominence, Time, Intermittent reminders — Student: Drill, Fast pace, Independent practice	Instruction imbedded in other activities / Natural antecedents / High utility / Natural consequences
Content	Introduction and Practice With . . . / Definitions / Concepts characteristics / Procedures	Additional Practice With . . . / Definitions / Concepts characteristics / Procedures	Review of . . . / Definitions / Concepts characteristics / Procedures	Applications of . . . / Definitions / Concepts characteristics / Procedures
Measurement	Accuracy / Frequency of correct responses/errors	Accuracy and Speed / Frequency of correct responses/ errors / Rate of responding	Accuracy and Speed / Frequency of correct responses/errors / Rate of responding	Accuracy and Speed / Frequency of correct responses/errors / Rate of responding
Cue	Do It	Do It Faster	Use It or Lose It	Use It Again Somewhere Else

89

Chapter 7: Present Information

Strategy:	**Vary Opportunities for Practice**

Content Skills:	Arts; Fitness; Mathematics/Problem Solving/Calculating; Reading; Social Studies; Science; Writing
Learning Difference:	Attention; Study Skills; Processing Verbal Information; Cognition High; Cognition Low; Mobility; Hearing; Health; Cognition Mixed; Memory Short-Term; Memory Long-Term; Seeing; Speaking/Talking; Fine Motor (handwriting, articulation, etc.); Gross Motor (running, walking, etc.); Processing Visual Information; Processing Verbal Information; Receptive Language/Decoding (listening, reading); Expressive Language/ Encoding (speaking, writing, spelling); Social Knowledge; Self-Control; Social Behaviors; Self-Confidence; Self-Care
Disability Category:	Attention Deficit/Hyperactivity Disorder; Visual Impairments; Deafness/Blindness; Gifted and Talented; Hearing Impairments; Mental Retardation; Multiple Disabilities; Traumatic Brain Injury; Second Language Learning Needs; Serious Emotional Disturbance; Specific Learning Disabilities; Speech or Language Impairments; Orthopedic or Other Health Impairments; Autism

Tactic Title:	**Using a Homework Agenda**

Problem:	Frequently, students with a disability have difficulty sustaining attention and staying on-task in the classroom. Consequently, they may not record homework assignments accurately. Unfortunately, they are then unable to practice their classroom learning at other times and in other settings—a condition that is essential for their being able to become proficient and to maintain and generalize their learning. Bottom line: They are unable to complete assignments completely and/or accurately.
Tactic:	Supply students with student planners for their personal use as a "Homework Agenda" (see the following Homework Agenda). If your school/district does not provide planners, simply ask students to designate a notebook for this purpose. When assigning homework, be sure that students write these assignments in their Agendas; let students work in pairs to ensure that they have recorded your instructions correctly. Allow time for their questions and ensure they make the necessary corrections before they leave your classroom. Have peers (or you) initial that the assignment is entered correctly. Upon completion of the assignment at home, have the student's parents initial as well.
Example:	Having my students understand and record homework assignments accurately is so essential for every student . . . especially those with special needs. Parent signatures are essential as well, and I call home every now and then to be sure we are all on the same track. We're now in the

process of refining our "Homework Hotline," where students/parents can call in to double-check on assignments. . . . Trying to make it more interactive.

Abby A., teacher

Benefits: Using homework agendas

- ensures that students have accurate and varied ways to practice skills they are learning or need to maintain;
- invokes responsibility and organization of materials; and
- improves student learning and achievement.

Literature: Anhalt, K., McNeil, C. B., & Bahl, A. B. (1998). The ADHD classroom kit: A whole classroom approach for managing disruptive behavior. *Psychology in the Schools, 35*(1), 67–77.

Homework Agenda

Content Area:	Assignment:	Date Given:	Due:

Chapter 7: Present Information

Strategy:	Vary Methods of Practice

Content Skills:	Writing; Science; Reading; Mathematics/Problem Solving/Calculating

Learning Difference:	Mobility; Speaking/Talking; Attention; Expressive Language/Encoding (speaking, writing, spelling); Fine Motor (handwriting, articulation, etc.); Gross Motor (running, walking, etc.); Self-Confidence; Receptive Language/Decoding (listening, reading); Processing Verbal Information; Processing Visual Information

Disability Category:	Multiple Disabilities; Orthopedic or Other Health Impairments; Visual Impairments; Hearing Impairments; Traumatic Brain Injury

Tactic Title:	Using Assistive Technology in Writing Tasks

Problem:	Students with disabilities in communication and mobility (both gross and fine motor), as well as receptive and expressive language, need modified forms of instruction to benefit fully from instruction.

Tactic:	For students who have limited communication or mobility, tailor their lessons so they can remain actively engaged. In planning instruction, take into account their abilities, as well as their limitations. To aid students with writing, consider assistive technology (AT). Students can use trackball mice on computers to assist their fine motor control, while simultaneously making use of software programs such as Discovery and Word Prediction, which reduce the number of keystrokes the student must make. Others with speech limitations can use communication boards to tell instructional aides what to write down on the test. Some students use grids that help them stay on the lines when writing. Teachers can also use videos, overheads, PowerPoint presentations, and other forms of assistive technology that incorporate audio, visual, and hands-on activities to keep the students engaged.

Example:	With the help of our technology specialist and the special education staff, I have seen the benefits of AT firsthand. I really rely on them to match the technology to the individual student; I couldn't possibly know all the options on my own. Also, the IEP spells out the AT that should be used. One thing I've learned is that AT can be as simple as a rubber gripper on a pen; it doesn't always have to be a complicated piece of equipment or an expensive software program. In fact, I use many of the built-in features of my word processing program, such as enlarging font sizes, color coding, voice-over, zooming, visual and auditory alerts, sticky keys, as well as modified cursor size and speed. Most of the AT is just common sense and, in fact, works for many of my other students as well.

Sebastion R., teacher

Benefits: Making appropriate use of assistive technology

- enables students to become more self-sufficient and independent;
- provides teachers with additional tools to use in teaching and monitoring student learning; and
- makes learning equitable for all students.

Literature: Behrmann, M. M., & Jerome, M. K. (2002). *Assistive technology for students with mild disabilities: Update 2002* (ERIC Digest E623). Arlington, VA: ERIC Clearinghouse on Disabilities and Gifted Education, Council for Exceptional Children. (ERIC Document Reproduction Service No. ED463595)

Ford, D. Y., & Harris III, J. J. (1999). *Multicultural gifted education.* New York: Teachers College Press.

Chapter 7: Present Information

Strategy:	Monitor Amount of Work Assigned
Content Skills:	Arts; Fitness; Mathematics/Problem Solving/Calculating; Reading; Social Studies; Science; Writing
Learning Difference:	Cognition High; Cognition Low; Cognition Mixed; Attention; Processing Visual Information; Memory Short-Term; Memory Long-Term; Receptive Language/Decoding (listening, reading); Processing Verbal Information; Study Skills; Social Knowledge; Self-Control; Social Behaviors; Self-Confidence; Mobility; Hearing; Health; Seeing; Speaking/Talking; Fine Motor (handwriting, articulation, etc.); Gross Motor (running, walking, etc.); Expressive Language/Encoding (speaking, writing, spelling); Self-Care
Disability Category:	Attention Deficit/Hyperactivity Disorder; Orthopedic or Other Health Impairments; Autism; Second Language Learning Needs; Serious Emotional Disturbance; Specific Learning Disabilities; Speech or Language Impairments; Traumatic Brain Injury; Multiple Disabilities; Mental Retardation; Hearing Impairments; Gifted and Talented; Deafness/Blindness; Visual Impairments

Tactic Title:	Grouping to Monitor Student Learning More Efficiently
Problem:	With large numbers of students, limited instructional time, and diverse abilities and needs, it is essential for teachers to find ways to provide as much individual attention as possible, while monitoring the appropriateness of assigned tasks. Are they too difficult? Too easy? Too lengthy? Too short?
Tactic:	Divide students into groups to complete assignments; this tactic takes the focus off you as the only source of information and creates more efficient instructional time for students. As students are working, you can move around your room observing students, providing assistance, monitoring the appropriateness of the work you have assigned, and making modifications when needed. For example, you can reduce the number of problems, provide a supplemental task for those finishing before others, and select certain students to work with others. As you constantly check on the progress of individual students' performance, you have the freedom to structure, manage, and pace all activities taking place in your classroom simultaneously.
Example:	Of course, I would like to have small class sizes, but that's not going to happen. So I've moved away from the lecture (teacher-centered) instructional format to small-group (student-centered) learning. Students come to class having read the text for homework. So we have a brief discussion

or reflection time so they can ask questions or share their opinions. Then I give them the problem for the day, and they move into their small groups for most of the period. I work with my special education teacher and her paraprofessional to arrange groups of diverse learners, because learning cooperatively is a lifelong skill. The students seem to enjoy my classes, but I have to admit, we're not always the quietest class on this hall.

Maci T., teacher

Benefits: Dividing the class into smaller, workable groups provides

- the teacher the opportunity to monitor individual students and their progress;
- additional instructional time that can be used for advance instruction or activities and in-depth exploration of content areas; and
- opportunities for greater coverage of content and, to some extent, greater in-depth treatment of content.

Literature: Zahorik, J. A. (1999). Reducing class size leads to individualized instruction. *Educational Leadership, 57*(1), 50–53.

8

Monitor Presentations

Principle	Strategy
Monitor Presentations	*Providing Feedback*
	Give Immediate, Frequent, Explicit Feedback
	Provide Specific Praise and Encouragement
	Model Correct Performance
	Provide Prompts and Cues
	Check Student Understanding
	Keeping Students Actively Involved
	Monitor Performance Regularly
	Monitor Performance During Practice
	Use Peers to Improve Instruction
	Provide Opportunities for Success
	Limit Opportunities for Failure
	Monitor Engagement Rates

Chapter 8: Monitor Presentations

Strategy:	**Give Immediate, Frequent, Explicit Feedback**
Content Skills:	Writing; Science; Social Studies; Reading; Mathematics/Problem Solving/Calculating; Arts; Fitness
Learning Difference:	Attention; Processing Visual Information; Study Skills; Social Knowledge; Self-Control; Memory Short-Term; Receptive Language/ Decoding (listening, reading); Self-Confidence
Disability Category:	Autism; Visual Impairments; Deafness/Blindness; Hearing Impairments; Mental Retardation; Multiple Disabilities; Traumatic Brain Injury; Serious Emotional Disturbance; Specific Learning Disabilities; Speech or Language Impairments; Attention Deficit/Hyperactivity Disorder; Orthopedic or Other Health Impairments

Tactic Title:	**Using an Assignment Schedule**
Problem:	Many students with disabilities struggle to remain focused and complete tasks when they are unsure of assignments.
Tactic:	First, use an Assignment Schedule (see page 100) to outline the tasks for one class period. Fill out the schedule prior to class or with the student and review it. This will give you an opportunity to explain tasks and expectations to students and give students an opportunity to use their communication skills. Break down the activities within each subject area so that students can follow along easily and check off each task when it is completed. Be sure that students understand what they are supposed to do. Tell students to place the Schedule in a visible place where they are working. Then, as you circulate around the classroom and monitor students, use the Comments section of the Assignment Schedule to provide ongoing feedback, suggestions, or ideas that let the student know how he or she is doing. Finally, at the end of the class period, take a moment to review the Schedule together, discuss any issues regarding student's work reflected on the schedule, and plan for the next step. Both you and the student initial the document.
Example:	I use Assignment Schedules with several students at once, and I let my students make comments as well . . . sometimes they just write "Help!" It's a nice way to communicate without disrupting the learning of other students. I see them starting to take more responsibility for their learning. Right now, they like me to make comments several times during a class, but as they gain more confidence, I'll move to other, less concrete and more natural types of feedback (a smile, nod, thumbs up . . . something that I would use with any student.

Juliette M., teacher

Benefits: Assignment schedules

- make students aware of teacher expectations;
- provide a way for students to monitor their own progress during a task;
- reduce disruptive behavior; and
- enable teachers to provide immediate, supportive, and/or correct feedback.

Literature: Dollard, N. (1996). Constructive classroom management. *Focus on Exceptional Children, 29,* 1–12.

Assignment Schedule

Name:_____   Date:_____   Class:_____

Time:	Assignment:	Comments:	Initials:

Signatures: Student _____ Teacher _____

Chapter 8: Monitor Presentations

Strategy:	**Provide Specific Praise and Encouragement**
Content Skills:	Arts; Fitness; Mathematics/Problem Solving/Calculating; Reading; Social Studies; Science; Writing
Learning Difference:	Self-Control; Processing Visual Information; Memory Long-Term; Receptive Language/Decoding (listening, reading); Expressive Language/Encoding (speaking, writing, spelling); Social Behaviors; Self-Confidence; Attention; Cognition Low; Hearing; Health; Cognition Mixed; Memory Short-Term; Speaking/Talking; Study Skills; Fine Motor (handwriting, articulation, etc.); Gross Motor (running, walking, etc.); Processing Verbal Information; Social Knowledge
Disability Category:	Serious Emotional Disturbance; Attention Deficit/Hyperactivity Disorder; Specific Learning Disabilities; Second Language Learning Needs; Speech or Language Impairments; Traumatic Brain Injury; Mental Retardation; Autism

Tactic Title:	**Using Constructive and Encouraging Feedback**
Problem:	Some students with disabilities tend to take criticism, suggestions, corrections, and negative feedback very poorly. They may feel inferior or misunderstood, or they may simply not understand what is required.
Tactic:	Provide as many opportunities as possible for students to correct or modify assignments prior to submitting a final version to you. Drafts and extra practice examples help to eliminate misconceptions. Insist that students use the complete time to finish assignments and discourage rushing to get done fast. Stress that accuracy is more important than finishing first. When correcting assignments, try to point out more positive elements than negative ones and make clear, insightful comments while editing copy. The clearer the comments, the fewer misconceptions a student will have. Provide opportunities for students to discuss their work with you privately, for many of these children do not like to be identified as a failure in front of the whole class. Use a rubric to guide your grading. Compliment students on their "dedication to accuracy" and provide opportunities for extra credit to those who really do try hard. Allow for make-ups on tests with consistent errors, skipped questions, and misnumbering.
Example:	I know some students have greater difficulty with being corrected; we all like being right. So, it's really important for me to emphasize the positive. I find something nice to say first, even if it's just "Nice shirt!"

Seriously, I've learned to provide grading rubrics *beforehand,* so my students know exactly what I expect. Rubrics also give me specific items that I can praise before moving on to errors or suggestions for improvement.

Bonnie O., teacher

Benefits:

Teachers who use praise and encouragement

- reduce their students' feelings of helplessness and confusion;
- build their students' self-confidence and emphasis on accuracy; and
- increase their students' willingness to take risks and try.

Literature:

Arntz, A. (1993). Treatment of borderline personality disorder: A challenge for cognitive-behavioral therapy. *Behavioral Research Therapy, 32,* 419–430.

Chapter 8: Monitor Presentations

Strategy:	**Model Correct Performance**
Content Skills:	Science; Writing; Social Studies; Mathematics/Problem Solving/ Calculating; Reading
Learning Difference:	Study Skills; Receptive Language/Decoding (listening, reading); Expressive Language/Encoding (speaking, writing, spelling); Fine Motor (handwriting, articulation, etc.); Hearing; Processing Verbal Information; Processing Verbal Information
Disability Category:	Specific Learning Disabilities; Visual Impairments; Mental Retardation; Traumatic Brain Injury; Second Language Learning Needs; Serious Emotional Disturbance; Speech or Language Impairments; Attention Deficit/Hyperactivity Disorder; Orthopedic or Other Health Impairments; Autism

Tactic Title:	**Modeling Note Taking**
Problem:	Frequently, students with learning disabilities have difficulty listening to a class lecture and taking coherent, legible handwritten notes simultaneously. Subsequently, they may have difficulty understanding their own notes while completing assignments or preparing for tests.
Tactic:	When the special education teacher is coteaching, share responsibility for the entire class period. You might introduce the lesson and lecture. While you are talking, the special education teacher outlines the important points with supporting notes on the overhead or whiteboard. In other words, he or she models note taking so that the notes are visible to all students. They see a real example of how to take notes that they can copy if need be. After the lecture, you both move around the classroom as students work in their small groups. At the end of the period, the special education teacher does the closure and provides feedback. You both make sure that students have recorded the important points in their notes. You also post the notes on the class Web site so that students can revise their notes and use the teacher's notes to review for tests. Then you distribute the homework assignment and dismiss the class when the bell rings. The next day, reverse the roles.
Example:	My teaching partner and I use a computer and projector to model note taking for our students. Most either take notes on their own or copy the notes we write. There are one or two students who simply cannot take written notes due to their disabilities, so we print copies for them as soon as we can. As we are taking notes, we often stop to point out why we underlined a certain phrase or how the three subtopics fit logically under the main topic. We've developed our own form of "shorthand" abbreviations: "tx" for *teach* or *teacher*, "lx" for *learner*, "dx" for *disability*.

Of course, we make sure that they know the correct spelling. Note taking is such an important skill for them to have, it's worth taking the time to teach it.

Mark D., teacher

Benefits: By modeling note taking, teachers

- reduce the risk that students will practice errors, lack information, or misinterpret content;
- provide a lifelong skill that is applicable across content areas and situations; and
- enhance students' organization of information and comprehension.

Literature: Behrmann, M. M. (1995). *Assistive technology for students with mild disabilities* (ERIC Digest E529). Reston, VA: ERIC Clearinghouse on Disabilities and Gifted Education, Council for Exceptional Children. (ERIC Document Reproduction Service No. ED378755)

Biddulph, G., Hess, P., & Humes, R. (2006). Helping a child with learning challenges be successful in the general education classroom. *Intervention in School & Clinic, 41,* 315–316.

Friend, M., & Bursuck, W. D. (2009). *Including students with special needs: A practical guide for teachers.* Boston: Allyn & Bacon.

Chapter 8: Monitor Presentations

Strategy:	Provide Prompts and Cues
Content Skills:	Reading; Social Studies; Science; Mathematics/Problem Solving/Calculating; Arts; Fitness
Learning Difference:	Attention; Study Skills; Receptive Language/Decoding (listening, reading); Expressive Language/Encoding (speaking, writing, spelling); Social Behaviors; Cognition Mixed; Processing Verbal Information; Processing Visual Information; Memory Short-Term; Memory Long-Term; Cognition High; Cognition Low
Disability Category:	Serious Emotional Disturbance; Visual Impairments; Deafness/Blindness; Gifted and Talented; Hearing Impairments; Mental Retardation; Multiple Disabilities; Traumatic Brain Injury; Second Language Learning Needs; Specific Learning Disabilities; Speech or Language Impairments; Attention Deficit/Hyperactivity Disorder; Orthopedic or Other Health Impairments; Autism

Tactic Title:	Teaching a Contextual Clue Strategy Using Embedded Foreign Words
Problem:	All students may have trouble understanding new vocabulary in reading assignments, but for students with disabilities, encountering new words may prove to be distracting and confusing, as well as frustrating.
Tactic:	Select a story such as "Two Dreamers" by Gary Soto (2000), a story that incorporates Spanish words (reading level: Grade 6). Introduce the story and tell students that there will be foreign words in the story. As the students read the story, ask the students what the foreign words might mean in a particular sentence. Encourage students to use the previous contextual information and the rest of the sentence to guess the meaning of the word. Use the Contextual Clue Worksheet to record their thinking. When the students approximate the English word for the foreign counterpart, provide positive reinforcement.
Example:	We have a lot of students who are learning English in our school in addition to students with language disabilities. So this tactic is a wonderful way to teach them to use context clues, while expanding their vocabulary in at least one language. I've let my students create their own stories and replace familiar words with the foreign counterparts. I like to create pairs of learners whose native languages are not the same.

Jessica P., teacher

Benefits: Using context clues as prompts and cues

- encourages students to think critically;
- can be applied across categories of disabilities, languages, and content areas; and
- expands comprehension and use of new vocabulary.

Literature: Ward-Lonergan, J. M., Liles, B. Z., & Owen, S. V. (1996). Contextual strategy instruction: Socially/emotionally maladjusted adolescents with language impairments. *Journal of Communication Disorders, 29,* 107–124.

Contextual Clue Sheet

Title of Story:_____ **Author:**_____

Foreign Word	Context	Translation

Chapter 8: Monitor Presentations

Strategy:	**Check Student Understanding**

Content Skills:	Writing; Social Studies
Learning Difference:	Expressive Language/Encoding (speaking, writing, spelling); Attention; Cognition Mixed; Memory Short-Term; Memory Long-Term; Study Skills; Fine Motor (handwriting, articulation, etc.); Processing Visual Information; Processing Verbal Information; Receptive Language/ Decoding (listening, reading); Self-Confidence
Disability Category:	Specific Learning Disabilities; Serious Emotional Disturbance; Second Language Learning Needs; Speech or Language Impairments; Attention Deficit/Hyperactivity Disorder; Mental Retardation; Traumatic Brain Injury

Tactic Title:	**Student-Created Rubrics for Writing Evaluation**

Problem:	Writing is an individualistic process, and teachers may find that for learners with language disabilities, it is difficult to determine the criteria for assessing an essay in a way that would encourage students in their progress.
Tactic:	Allow students to have input on a rubric designed to assess their writing. Before a student begins to write an essay, hold a conference with the student. Working together, ask the student to identify the point of writing the essay described and to identify strengths and weaknesses in his or her own writing. As the student mentions each item, write down the responses and incorporate them into an individualized rubric for the assignment. Discuss what is required to be successful for each of the rubric items. Determine point values for each item or another method of scoring the rubric. Highlight the most important points for the student to focus on in when writing. Then the student writes essay with these points in mind. When the essay is to be graded, complete a rubric and ask the student to complete one as well. Then meet again and discuss the similarities and differences between the two rubrics and agree on a final grade. Using pre- and postconferences enables you to check for student understanding throughout the process.
Example:	This tactic is an excellent way for students to see clearly what they are expected to do. They also are active participants in evaluating their work on the agreed-upon criteria. I take it one step further. After writing the essay, I ask them to reflect on specific questions, such as these: What do you want your reader to learn from your essay? Is there a spot that is confusing? Then we have our postconference and outline objectives for the next assignment.

Marilyn P., teacher

Benefits: When students create and score their own scoring rubrics,

- their writing is more focused and guided;
- they gain a sense of control over their writing; and
- they learn to think critically about their work.

Literature: Jackson, C. W., & Larkin, M. J. (2002). Rubrics: Teaching students to use grading rubrics. *Teaching Exceptional Children, 35*(1), 40–45.

Chapter 8: Monitor Presentations

Strategy:	**Monitor Performance Regularly**

Content Skills: Arts; Mathematics/Problem Solving/Calculating; Reading; Social Studies; Science

Learning Difference: Expressive Language/Encoding (speaking, writing, spelling); Fine Motor (handwriting, articulation, etc.); Attention; Cognition High; Cognition Low; Mobility; Hearing; Health; Cognition Mixed; Memory Short-Term; Seeing; Memory Long-Term; Speaking/Talking; Study Skills; Processing Visual Information; Processing Verbal Information; Receptive Language/Decoding (listening, reading); Social Knowledge; Self-Confidence

Disability Category: Specific Learning Disabilities; Visual Impairments; Deafness/Blindness; Gifted and Talented; Hearing Impairments; Mental Retardation; Multiple Disabilities; Traumatic Brain Injury; Serious Emotional Disturbance; Speech or Language Impairments; Attention Deficit/Hyperactivity Disorder; Orthopedic or Other Health Impairments; Autism

Tactic Title:	**Using Journals to Gauge Student Understanding**

Problem: It is often frustrating when students do not contribute or participate actively in a large group discussion. Changing tendencies for a student to say, "I like what he said," or, "I think what she said," is challenging.

Tactic: Before beginning discussion on a given topic, pose a guiding question for students to enter in the journals. For example, you might ask: "What does the author suggest about the character's motivation for doing X?" or, "Given the political situation in _____, what is the role of the legislature?" Provide time for them to write down their responses. Then begin the discussion; the students' initial reactions will not be swayed by those of their peers. Encourage everyone to contribute. Finally, review journals to monitor students' understanding of your initial question. Journals need not be graded but used just to monitor and encourage student thinking and participation.

Example: I've always used student journals as a way for students to reflect on various topics—personal and academic. I'd just never thought of using them to encourage greater participation in discussions. However, I can see how they might think that their ideas have value and, having had the time to reflect on the question, be more likely to jump in to the discussion. At the very least, this tactic gets them thinking independently before hearing what their classmates think. By the way, I never grade journals; I want my students to be free to think and just write.

Xan T., teacher

Benefits: Using guiding questions and journals

- gives teachers an additional tool to monitor student understanding of the content;
- focuses student attention on a given topic; and
- lets students express their thoughts and ideas freely without being put "on the spot" while learning.

Literature: Chandler, A. (1997). Is this for a grade? A personal look at journals. *English Journal, 86,* 45–49.

Chapter 8: Monitor Presentations

Strategy:	**Monitor Performance During Practice**

Content Skills:	Arts; Mathematics/Problem Solving/Calculating; Reading; Social Studies; Science
Learning Difference:	Social Knowledge; Expressive Language/Encoding (speaking, writing, spelling); Cognition Low; Speaking/Talking; Social Behaviors
Disability Category:	Mental Retardation; Second Language Learning Needs; Serious Emotional Disturbance; Specific Learning Disabilities; Speech or Language Impairments; Attention Deficit/Hyperactivity Disorder; Autism; Traumatic Brain Injury

Tactic Title:	**Using Cooperative Groups**

Problem:	For many students with disabilities, being included in general education settings can be stressful. They are challenged not only by academic expectations but also by new social relationships. Many lack the social competence to know how to get along with their classmates.
Tactic:	To promote the development of social skills among students in your classes, use collaborative group activities. Prior to a lab class, choose groups of three students who have mixed cognitive abilities to facilitate learning for the students with lower cognitive ability and to teach the others about diversity. During the experiment, observe the interactions of the students with each other. For example, observe how the general education students try to include the special needs students and how the students with special needs respond to their peers' suggestions and instruction. You might record your observations on a Cooperative Group Observation Sheet. Individualize your assessments of student learning. For the general education students, use a combination of social skills and academic performance (worksheets, postexperiment quizzes, etc.). Assess the students with disability at their individual content ability level and emphasize the social skills they demonstrated and imitated within their designated group.
Example:	I'm very careful to assign roles when I use cooperative groups in my history classes. I assign the roles based on tasks at which students can succeed and learn. Students with higher ability might be notetakers, reporters, or organizers, while others could be timekeepers or responsible for collecting materials. I use the Cooperative Group Observation Sheet to record student interactions. We always take time after a cooperative group lesson to discuss how the groups "worked" . . . strategies they used, what they liked about it, what they learned, etc.

Barb A., teacher

Benefits:	Cooperative group activities

- enhance learning opportunities for all students;
- teach important social skills through imitation and practice;
- reinforce concepts as students discuss different ideas among the members of their group.

Literature: Farrel, M., & John, E. (1995). Literacy for all? The case of Down syndrome. *Journal of Reading, 38,* 270–280.

Nagel, P. (2008). Moving beyond lecture: Cooperative learning and the secondary social studies classroom. *Education, 128,* 363–368.

Cooperative Group Observation Sheet

Group #/Name:_____

Enter students' names inside the boxes and record observations.

Group #/Name:_____

Enter students' names inside the boxes and record observations.

Group #/Name:_____

Enter students' names inside the boxes and record observations.

Group #/Name:_____

Enter students' names inside the boxes and record observations.

Chapter 8: Monitor Presentations

Strategy:	Use Peers to Improve Instruction
Content Skills:	Mathematics/Problem Solving/Calculating
Learning Difference:	Social Knowledge; Expressive Language/Encoding (speaking, writing, spelling); Cognition Low; Speaking/Talking; Social Behaviors
Disability Category:	Mental Retardation; Second Language Learning Needs; Serious Emotional Disturbance; Specific Learning Disabilities; Speech or Language Impairments; Attention Deficit/Hyperactivity Disorder; Autism; Traumatic Brain Injury

Tactic Title:	Using Peers to Solve Complex Problems (Not Just in Math)
Problem:	Frequently, students have difficulty understanding higher-level concepts and seeing their real-life applications.
Tactic:	Real-life examples and clear instructions are essential in these instances. First, pair students in carefully planned groups of two or three. Then present a problem that involves higher-level thinking skills related to a specific mathematical problem/equation. Provide a list of possible locations, people, and resources that might help them answer the problem. For example, in working with quadratic equations, you might suggest measuring and comparing the dimensions/area of your classroom as compared to the cafeteria, parking lot, or soccer field. Send them off on a scavenger hunt (field trip) around your school to collect the data needed to answer the problem. Have students record their findings in their math journals, being careful to note the specific problem, exact date, and data/artifact they collected/observed. Finally, each pair makes a presentation to their classmates in which they demonstrate their data, conclusions, and strategies used to solve the problem.
Example:	I just love using problems that represent real applications of what I am trying to teach. Having students figure out how to solve these problems together just adds another layer of reality to the mix. I am very careful in my planning my small groups; I need to place students with others who can supplement and support their academic and social strengths and needs. Sometimes our "field trips/scavenger hunts" are virtual; we use the Internet, especially MapQuest, a lot. Their presentations have been phenomenal and make wonderful contributions to their portfolios, especially for those with IEPs. I can see my colleagues in other subject areas using this tactic as well.

Andres T., teacher

Benefits: Pairing students in activities

- teaches both academic and social skills;
- teaches students the value of collaboration and colleagues in solving problems; and
- is applicable across content areas, categories of disability, learning differences, and grade levels.

Literature: Hurd, D. W. (1997). Novelty and its relation to field trips. *Education, 118,* 29–35.

Stenhoff, D. M., & Lignugaris, B. (2007). A review of the effects of peer tutoring on students with mild disabilities in secondary settings. *Exceptional Children, 74,* 8–30.

Chapter 8: Monitor Presentations

Strategy:	Provide Opportunities for Success
Content Skills:	Arts; Fitness; Mathematics/Problem Solving/Calculating; Reading; Social Studies; Science; Writing
Learning Difference:	Self-Control; Attention; Cognition Low; Cognition High; Cognition Mixed; Study Skills
Disability Category:	Attention Deficit/Hyperactivity Disorder; Visual Impairments; Deafness/Blindness; Gifted and Talented; Hearing Impairments; Mental Retardation; Multiple Disabilities; Traumatic Brain Injury; Second Language Learning Needs; Serious Emotional Disturbance; Specific Learning Disabilities; Speech or Language Impairments; Orthopedic or Other Health Impairments; Autism

Tactic Title:	Using Peers as Buddies
Problem:	Students often struggle with remaining focused and on-task during instruction. Teachers with the very best intentions also struggle with balancing precious time between instruction and managing behavior.
Tactic:	The peer buddy system can be used to address individual student needs and provide opportunities for successful learning. Pair a student with a disability with a peer without a disability (the peer buddy). Engage students in the selection process.
	Devise a checklist for the peer buddy to review at the beginning and end of class (see checklist on page 119). The checklist might include questions such as "Do you have all your books, papers, and a pencil or pen?" and "Do you know what tonight's homework assignment is?" Finally, monitor the actions of both students and the success of the system.
Example:	This is a great way to keep students actively involved with all classroom activities; it also makes teacher expectations clear to students. I can see how the general education students would learn responsibility and empathy, while the students with disabilities emulate their buddies positive behaviors, thus improving their interpersonal skills. I think it is important to provide time to train students how to be a peer buddy, perhaps through a trainer-of-trainers model, where one peer buddy teaches the next and so on.

Russ F., teacher

Benefits: The peer buddy system

- engages students in positive, productive learning behaviors;
- provides structure and support for the student with a disability; and
- encourages students to take responsibility and play an active role in their own learning.

Literature: Camoni, G. A., & McGeehan, L. (1997). Peer buddies: A child-to-child support program. *Principal, 76*, 40–43.

Peer Buddy System Checklist

Student Name: _____ **Date:**_____

Peer Buddy:_____

Teacher—Enter questions below:	**Student/Peer Buddy—Circle the correct response below:**

- _____ Yes/No

- _____ Yes/No

- _____ Yes/No

- _____ Yes/No

- _____ Yes/No

- _____ Yes/No

- _____ Yes/No

- _____ Yes/No

- _____ Yes/No

Signed by Student:_____ **Peer Buddy:**_____

Chapter 8: Monitor Presentations

Strategy:	**Limit Opportunities for Failure**
Content Skills:	Mathematics/Problem Solving/Calculating; Reading; Social Studies; Science; Writing; Arts; Fitness
Learning Difference:	Cognition Low; Attention; Processing Visual Information; Study Skills; Self-Control; Memory Short-Term; Receptive Language/Decoding (listening, reading); Expressive Language/Encoding (speaking, writing, spelling); Social Behaviors; Self-Confidence; Cognition High; Mobility; Hearing; Health; Cognition Mixed; Memory Long-Term; Seeing; Speaking/Talking; Fine Motor (handwriting, articulation, etc.); Gross Motor (running, walking, etc.); Processing Verbal Information; Social Knowledge; Self-Care
Disability Category:	Specific Learning Disabilities; Visual Impairments; Deafness/Blindness; Gifted and Talented; Hearing Impairments; Mental Retardation; Multiple Disabilities; Traumatic Brain Injury; Second Language Learning Needs; Serious Emotional Disturbance; Speech or Language Impairments; Attention Deficit/Hyperactivity Disorder; Orthopedic or Other Health Impairments; Autism

Tactic Title:	**Peer Tutoring in the Secondary Classroom**
Problem:	Teachers are often frustrated when they are not able to give individual attention to students with disabilities in their classrooms.
Tactic:	Peer tutoring is an effective tool in providing needed instruction to students with disabilities. First, identify students who would benefit from peer tutoring (tutees) and other students who would be good tutors. Identify the skill(s) to be tutored and develop a one-page tutoring guideline sheet for tutors to use when they are tutoring. (Based on your needs and classroom, you might list some of the following: Select a quiet corner of the classroom. Gather materials to be used. Provide instructions to your tutee; ask your tutee to repeat the instructions. Monitor tutoring time; at end of the tutoring session, ask the tutee to summarize what he or she has learned. Thank your tutee. Submit materials to the teacher.). Then train responsible, high-achieving students to serve as peer tutors. Provide a space or place for tutoring sessions. Finally, monitor interventions regularly to ensure that peer tutoring is benefiting both the tutor and the tutee.
Example:	This is a wonderful way for me to engage my higher-level students with others who need some additional support. It gives them an opportunity to review and refine their own learning as they teach others. It teaches them to be patient, understanding, and accepting. It's important to select the right tutors, train them well, and match the tutoring pairs

carefully. While this tactic frees up some of my time, I still have to monitor the tutoring sessions and make sure that the tutors are following the script.

Stan F., teacher

Benefits:

Using peers as tutors:

- provides reinforcement and review for tutors and individual attention for students with disabilities;
- is effective across grade levels, content areas, and categories of disability;
- increases opportunities for success and limits opportunities for failure; and
- assists students with disabilities in staying on-task, improving academic achievement, and improving study skills.

Literature:

Stenhoff, D. M., & Lignugaris, B. (2007). A review of the effects of peer tutoring on students with mild disabilities in secondary settings. *Exceptional Children, 74,* 8–30.

Chapter 8: Monitor Presentations

Strategy:	**Monitor Engagement Rates**
Content Skills:	Reading; Social Studies; Science
Learning Difference:	Attention; Processing Visual Information; Self-Control; Receptive Language/Decoding (listening, reading); Processing Verbal Information; Self-Confidence; Social Behaviors; Expressive Language/Encoding (speaking, writing, spelling); Processing Verbal Information; Cognition Low; Memory Short-Term; Memory Long-Term; Cognition Mixed; Study Skills
Disability Category:	Attention Deficit/Hyperactivity Disorder; Autism; Second Language Learning Needs; Serious Emotional Disturbance; Specific Learning Disabilities; Speech or Language Impairments; Traumatic Brain Injury; Mental Retardation

Tactic Title:	**Reading Aloud: Maintaining Attention and Building Confidence**
Problem:	Frequently, students with disabilities cannot concentrate in class, especially when an assignment requires reading because of their low level of reading ability.
Tactic:	Provide opportunities for students to read aloud in class as much as possible. Arrange students in small groups and have them read aloud to one another. Give students with reading disabilities time to read aloud to you. If their reading level is not high, read aloud to them so that they can hear the information and process it in an alternative fashion. Have the students point to the words you or they are reading so that they can keep track of where they are. If they lose track and their attention starts to wander, have them read aloud to you. They are less likely to lose concentration if they are encouraged to be active members of the class, rather than being punished. As the student remains involved in class activities, you can slowly incorporate them into the read-aloud group.
Example:	I've found that having students read their texts aloud to one another has all sorts of benefits. First, it gives them an opportunity to ask questions if they don't understand something; it has improved the accuracy and fluency and comprehension of some of my struggling readers. And it also gives me an opportunity to move around the room and monitor their participation, note their strengths and weaknesses, and clarify misunderstandings. When students are reading aloud in small groups or pairs, I can also spend time with individual students.

Joel S., teacher

Benefits: Providing time for students to read aloud
- encourages good reading habits;
- provides models of effective readers; and
- enables teachers to monitor student engagement.

Literature: Richardson, J. S. (2000). *Read it aloud: Using literature in the secondary content classroom.* Newark, DE: International Reading Association.

9

Adjust Presentations

Principle	Strategy
Adjust Presentations	Adapt Lessons to Meet Student Needs
	Provide Varied Instructional Options
	Alter Pace

Chapter 9: Adjust Presentations

Strategy:	Adapt Lessons to Meet Student Needs
Content Skills:	Mathematics/Problem Solving/Calculating; Reading; Social Studies; Writing; Science; Arts; Fitness
Learning Difference:	Speaking/Talking; Receptive Language/Decoding (listening, reading); Expressive Language/Encoding (speaking, writing, spelling); Fine Motor (handwriting, articulation, etc.); Attention; Cognition High; Cognition Mixed; Memory Short-Term; Study Skills; Processing Verbal Information
Disability Category:	Specific Learning Disabilities

Tactic Title:	Modifying Instructions
Problem:	Students with a learning disability frequently need additional supports to understand instructions and complete assignments.
Tactic:	Review all lesson plans before teaching students with learning disabilities to identify potential areas for modification. These students may need additional or more detailed instructions, instructions in both oral and written formats; or instructions broken down into separate parts. Many benefit from repetition, rehearsal, and visual cues. Review texts and other written material to identify ways to highlight organizational features, essential vocabulary, or cues. Collaborate with your special education teachers to identify the specific modifications and strategies that you can us to give your students with a learning disability a greater chance for success. Teachers enable students with learning disabilities to accomplish assigned tasks more successfully.
Example:	I think of the term *learning disability* as similar to having a "cold." Knowing that I have a "cold," by itself, does not tell me what to do. Just like the "common cold," which could mean I sneeze, or I cough, or I sneeze and cough, or I have a fever and sneeze—you get the idea. Just as there are many types of colds, there are many types of learning disabilities. One of my students, Taitia, has excellent oral language skills but can't write. Another, Julio, has fabulous ideas and writes well, but he spells at a Grade 3 level. Very challenging, but once we find the strategies and modifications that work for them, we're all fine. (They also work for other students without a disability, too!) If we (the teachers) don't know what to do, I just ask the student. Sometimes parents can be a wonderful resource. After all, they've known their child longer than any of us here. *Wendy P., teacher*

Benefits: Instructional modifications and adaptations

- provide the scaffolding to understanding that students with learning disabilities need;
- can be applied across lessons and content areas and students; and
- can be integrated into assessments as well.

Literature: Fuchs. L. S., & Fuchs, D. (1998). General educators' instructional adaptation for students with learning disabilities. *Learning Disability Quarterly, 221*, 23–33.

Chapter 9: Adjust Presentations

Strategy:	**Provide Varied Instructional Options**
Content Skills:	Mathematics/Problem Solving/Calculating; Reading; Social Studies; Writing; Science; Arts; Fitness
Learning Difference:	Attention; Fine Motor (handwriting, articulation, etc.); Study Skills; Processing Verbal Information; Receptive Language/Decoding (listening, reading)
Disability Category:	Attention Deficit/Hyperactivity Disorder; Mental Retardation; Traumatic Brain Injury; Second Language Learning Needs; Serious Emotional Disturbance; Specific Learning Disabilities; Speech or Language Impairments

Tactic Title:	**Modifying Test Formats for Students With Disabilities**
Problem:	Some students with disabilities may have difficulty maintaining their focus during tests.
Tactic:	First, develop a test for the general population of the class. Next, review the test and look for areas that may be problematic for students with various disabilities. These areas may include multiple-choice questions with too many choices, open-ended short answer questions that are too broad, or questions that may require drawing and labeling diagrams. Adjust these problem areas by providing extra supports within each section. These supports could include eliminating some of the choices in the multiple-choice questions, telling the students how many details to include in their answers to the short answer questions, or providing diagrams that are already drawn so that the students only has to label the picture. Finally, compare the two versions of the test to make sure they are assessing similar skills and degrees of knowledge.
Example:	I think that this is a good tactic for students who have a difficult time with attention. It makes it a lot easier for them to focus on the content rather than being distracted by multiple-choice questions that are too wordy or by excessively broad essay questions. However, if the questions are too wordy or broad, perhaps they should be modified for the entire class rather than just one student—just a thought. *Isiah T., teacher*
Benefits:	Creating modified tests • enables students with disabilities to demonstrate their knowledge more accurately, because the supports inherent in the tests help them stay interested and on-task;

- results in accurate data to support future planning, instruction, and assignments; and
- enhances students' motivation, because they know they will be evaluated fairly.

Literature: DuPaul, G. J., & Stoner, G. (1994). *ADHD in the schools: Assessment and intervention strategies.* New York: Guilford.

Chapter 9: Adjust Presentations

Strategy:	Alter Pace
Content Skills:	Mathematics/Problem Solving/Calculating; Reading; Social Studies; Science; Writing; Arts; Fitness
Learning Difference:	Attention; Self-Control; Study Skills; Social Behaviors; Self-Confidence; Processing Verbal Information; Receptive Language/Decoding (listening, reading); Expressive Language/Encoding (speaking, writing, spelling); Processing Visual Information
Disability Category:	Attention Deficit/Hyperactivity Disorder; Autism; Serious Emotional Disturbance; Specific Learning Disabilities; Traumatic Brain Injury; Second Language Learning Needs

Tactic Title:	Keeping Students With Disabilities on Track
Problem:	Teachers often find that students with disabilities become distracted and lose confidence when facing a difficult task or a series of assignments.
Tactic:	Provide interesting and appropriate assignments for all students, especially those with short attention spans or low tolerance for frustration. If students' attention starts drifting, break the assignment up into sections. When students complete each section, allow them to take a short break. Make academic tasks briefer; provide immediate and ongoing feedback about the accuracy of the assignment to stimulate attention and motivation to finish. Also, alternate active and passive tasks. When the entire assignment is complete, allow students to take a little longer break, because they will need it!
Example:	I think this is an excellent, appropriate tactic, involving goals and breaks in instruction so students can relax and refocus energies. Don't we all need and benefit from "breaks"? I also include my students in taking responsibility for planning out the day's activities. They like choices. They know everything must be done, but some need some flexibility in how it's all scheduled; it's just reasonable. Sometimes I just give two tasks and let them complete them in the order they prefer.

Isabel C., teacher

Benefits:	Altering the pace of instruction or assignments

- reduces frustration;
- increases motivation and self-confidence; and
- enables students with disabilities to stay on-task and be able to finish assigned tasks.

Literature:	Beringer, V. W. (1997). Introduction to interventions for students with learning and behavior problems: Myths and realities. *School Psychology Review, 26,* 326–332.

Evaluating Instruction

Effective teachers continuously monitor their students' understanding of the content being presented. They also monitor their students' use of instructional time to maximize their active engagement in appropriate learning activities. They keep records of progress and use the data to make decisions. In this part, we describe evidence-based strategies for each principle of evaluating instruction.

Component	Principle	Strategy
Evaluating Instruction (Part IV)	Monitor Student Understanding (Chapter 10)	Check Understanding of Directions Check Procedural Understanding Monitor Student Success Rate
	Monitor Engaged Time (Chapter 11)	Check Student Participation Teach Students to Monitor Their Own Participation
	Keep Records of Student Progress (Chapter 12)	Teach Students to Chart Their Own Progress Regularly Inform Students of Performance Maintain Records of Student Performance
	Use Data to Make Decisions (Chapter 13)	Use Data to Decide if More Services Are Warranted Use Student Progress to Make Teaching Decisions Use Student Progress to Decide When to Discontinue Services

Evaluating Instruction Works: A Case Study

In addition to being a history teacher, I am also the high school basketball coach. I often use the rules/format of basketball to assist students in review before an assessment. This allows individuals the opportunity to be part of one of two teams, and the goal of the game is to work together, just like in basketball, to come up with the most clear and accurate answer. I use an egg timer to keep track of the time, and the teams make baskets or score points each time an answer is clear and accurate. If the first team given the questions does not answer correctly, it is turned over to the other team. I found it interesting that one of my students always knew the most minute details during the basketball review. Then the next day during the test, she would barely pass. Upon further inquiry, this student was tested once accommodations for anxiety were put into place (writing in one color ink in class during assessment and another color at home) were unsuccessful. The student was identified as having dyslexia, and after she was given oral exams, she was able to answer the questions with newfound success and her grades dramatically increased. It is important to remember that when appropriate means are used to assist students in demonstrating their strengths, they do. While students are responding, I use an observation sheet like the grid in the book to jot down notes and observations related to the students and their performance on the review. This allows me the opportunity to monitor student growth, assist students who may be struggling, and plan for future instruction. (Related tactic is located in Chapter 12: Keep Records of Student Progress under Strategy: Maintain Records of Student Performance.)

10

Monitor Student Understanding

Principle	Strategy
Monitor Student Understanding	Check Understanding of Directions
	Check Procedural Understanding
	Monitor Student Success Rate

Chapter 10: Monitor Student Understanding

Strategy:	**Check Understanding of Directions**

Content Skills: Arts; Fitness; Mathematics/Problem Solving/Calculating; Reading; Social Studies; Science; Writing

Learning Difference: Study Skills; Receptive Language/Decoding (listening, reading); Expressive Language/Encoding (speaking, writing, spelling); Processing Verbal Information; Processing Visual Information

Disability Category: Mental Retardation; Traumatic Brain Injury; Serious Emotional Disturbance; Specific Learning Disabilities; Speech or Language Impairments; Attention Deficit/Hyperactivity Disorder; Autism

Tactic Title:	**Promoting Understanding, Learning, and Task Completion**

Problem: Often, individuals with disabilities may seem to be "misbehaving" when, quite simply, they did not understand or process instructions completely.

Tactic: First, when giving an assignment to your students, give instructions in the clearest language possible. Ask students to repeat your instructions; repeat instructions if a student is not clear or correct. Second, carefully monitor students to ensure understanding and on-task behavior. Third, praise students for remaining on-task and working the Daily Progress Report and assignments/homework daily. Give students a homework organizer. This may be one that is supplied by your school, a small spiral notebook, or a set of pages stapled or three-hole punched to be inserted into a binder. (See Homework Assignments that follows.) to keep track of their assignments; include positive highlights from the day. Require parents or guardians to sign when the assignment has been completed.

Example: We are so quick to assume that, once we've told the student what to do, they all "get it." . . . Not necessarily so, especially if you have students with disabilities related to processing verbal information or attention issues. I use the "see it, say it, repeat it" process. I provide instructions visually and verbally and ask the students to repeat the instructions. If we're dealing with homework, we add "write it" to the process, and by having them write instructions in their Homework Organizers. Often, we do a buddy check [see the "Using Peers as Buddies" tactic in Chapter 8] to be sure that everyone has it written correctly. This process prevents any number of potential "interruptions" to a student's learning. I've made sure that this process is included in IEPs, when needed. In that way, the process crosses classrooms with the students.

Vincent T., teacher

Benefits: Clarifying instructions immediately can

- provide students with a process and a structure for completing assignments successfully;
- encourage parents to become more involved and true partners their child's learning; and
- boost student self-confidence in the long run and motivate students to work well in other subjects, too.

Literature: Shima, K., & Gsovski, B. K. (1996). Making a way for Diana. *Educational Leadership, 53*(5), 37–40.

Daily Progress Report

Student Name: _____   **Date:** _____

Period	Subject	On Time	Had Supplies	Attentive	Participated	Had Homework	Teacher Initials	Comments

Homework Assignments

Title of Class: _____   Teacher: _____

Student: _____   Today's Date: _____

Title of Assignments: _____   Due Date: _____

Description of Assignment:

_____

_____

_____

_____

_____

_____

Resources:

_____

_____

Teacher Comments:

_____

_____

_____

Student Reflections:

_____

_____

_____

Parent Signature (when assignment has been completed):_____

Chapter 10: Monitor Student Understanding

Strategy:	**Check Procedural Understanding**

Content Skills: Arts; Fitness; Mathematics/Problem Solving/Calculating; Reading; Social Studies; Science; Writing

Learning Difference: Attention; Self-Control; Cognition Low; Cognition High; Hearing; Cognition Mixed; Memory Short-Term; Memory Long-Term; Speaking/Talking; Study Skills; Processing Visual Information; Processing Verbal Information; Receptive Language/Decoding (listening, reading); Expressive Language/Encoding (speaking, writing, spelling); Social Knowledge; Social Behaviors

Disability Category: Attention Deficit/Hyperactivity Disorder; Mental Retardation; Traumatic Brain Injury; Second Language Learning Needs; Serious Emotional Disturbance; Specific Learning Disabilities; Speech or Language Impairments; Autism

Tactic Title:	**Student Self-Management**

Problem: It is very frustrating when students do not follow established classroom procedures (such as homework submission, being on time, submitting written work, gaining the attention of the teacher, and basic classroom rules, for example). For many students, their apparent "noncompliance" is really a function of their disability. Therefore, they need additional tools to assist them in remembering and knowing how to adhere to classroom procedures.

Tactic: On the Classroom Procedures Checklist, beginning at the top of Column 2 (following "Date"), enter your classroom procedures. You might enter "comes to class on time," "completes homework," "stays on-task during class," and "raises hand to be called on" or whatever your own procedures are. Review procedures with students who are having difficulty following them and explain how you will all be using the check sheet to enable them to remember and follow procedures more successfully. Give each student a copy of the checklist; keep one for yourself. At the end of each class, you and the student check off each behavior that has been accomplished. Once the student consistently demonstrates success, you can stop filling out the checklist, with only the student required to complete it at the end of each class and show it to you. If the behavior continues to improve, the checklist can gradually be phased out, from every day to twice a week to once a week and, finally, not at all.

Example: The checklists take hardly any time at all to manage and they are teaching my students (only three or four of them) to take greater responsibility for themselves. Saves me a lot of time having to remind and remind them. I make it a little contest to see how many more times they agree with me each week. I require them to keep the check sheet in their homework planner so they can share with parents and their special education teacher. Finally, gives us hard data as a beginning point in planning.

Joshlyn W., teacher

Benefits: Careful monitoring of student understanding of classroom procedures

- reduces disruptions to instruction and learning;
- makes students more aware of behavior as the teacher sees it; and
- empowers them by giving them the tools to manage the behavior themselves.

Literature: Shapiro, E. S., DuPaul, G. J., & Bradley-Klug, K. L. (1998). Self-management as a strategy to improve the classroom behavior of adolescents with ADHD. *Journal of Learning Disabilities, 31*, 545–555.

Classroom Procedures Checklist

Student Name: _____

Date

Chapter 10: Monitor Student Understanding

Strategy:	Monitor Student Success Rate

Content Skills:	Reading; Social Studies; Science; Writing
Learning Difference:	Processing Visual Information; Memory Short-Term; Memory Long-Term; Receptive Language/Decoding (listening, reading); Expressive Language/Encoding (speaking, writing, spelling); Processing Verbal Information; Cognition High; Cognition Mixed; Cognition Low; Study Skills
Disability Category:	Specific Learning Disabilities; Mental Retardation; Second Language Learning Needs; Serious Emotional Disturbance; Speech or Language Impairments; Attention Deficit/Hyperactivity Disorder

Tactic Title:	Reader Response

Problem:	Students with learning disabilities often have trouble comprehending text they read and expressing themselves.
Tactic:	To monitor student comprehension and expression, use the reader response approach. Choose an article from the newspaper that you think students would find interesting and meaningful. For example, select an article dealing with anger and violence or a particularly relevant current event. Before the students read the article, ask them to discuss or write about their opinion regarding the topic from personal experience or perspective. You could ask: What makes people angry? Why is there so much violence in today's society? Does the media play too much of a role in politics? This allows students to draw on information they already know, which allows them to express themselves in a way that has meaning to them. Next, have the students read the article. After they have finished reading the article, ask them to write a brief summary of it. This allows you to monitor the students' understanding of the text and requires them to express themselves. Last, students could respond to this prompt: Write a brief personal reaction to the story/article you just read. Reread your thoughts on anger from the first question and draw some conclusions.
Example:	This is a way to teach students who have difficulty comprehending and expressing themselves! I especially like the idea of fostering prereading skills. Students tend to comprehend with greater understanding when I do something before reading that prepares them to understand the article. We keep their postreading thoughts in their journals as samples of thoughtful and informed reflection.
	Gregory Shafer (1997) provides valuable information on why reader response is a vital strategy to get students involved in their learning.

He gives an argument as to how this method of teaching gets students involved in their learning and makes it meaningful to them. He then goes on to describe how he used this method of teaching to teach a unit on the Civil War with his students. Throughout the unit, he is able to monitor the students' progress by looking at the various forms of response they provide him with. This is also how he critiques his teaching to make sure he is covering what he wants and that students are really getting the information. This article makes a good argument for why reader response is such a powerful tool to look at what you're doing as a teacher, what the students are actually learning, and finally how to teach students what you want in a way that is relevant to their lives.

Eduardo S., teacher

Benefits:

Using reader responses

- gives students an opportunity to express themselves on a topic with which they are familiar, making them active, rather than passive, participants in their learning;
- gives teachers evidence of how well students follow directions and how well they express themselves through writing; and
- provides information as to how teachers can adjust their own instruction to focus on specific student needs.

Literature:

Shafer, G. (1997). Reader response makes history. *English Journal, 86,* 65–68.

11

Monitor Engaged Time

Principle	Strategy
Monitor Engaged Time	Check Student Participation
	Teach Students to Monitor Their Own Participation

Chapter 11: Monitor Engaged Time

Strategy:	**Check Student Participation**

Content Skills: Arts; Fitness; Mathematics/Problem Solving/Calculating; Reading; Social Studies; Science; Writing

Learning Difference: Cognition High; Cognition Low; Cognition Mixed; Attention; Processing Visual Information; Memory Short-Term; Memory Long-Term; Receptive Language/Decoding (listening, reading); Processing Verbal Information; Study Skills; Social Knowledge; Self-Control; Social Behaviors; Self-Confidence; Mobility; Hearing; Health; Seeing; Speaking/Talking; Fine Motor (handwriting, articulation, etc.); Gross Motor (running, walking, etc.); Expressive Language/Encoding (speaking, writing, spelling); Self-Care

Disability Category: Attention Deficit/Hyperactivity Disorder; Orthopedic or Other Health Impairments; Autism; Second Language Learning Needs; Serious Emotional Disturbance; Specific Learning Disabilities; Speech or Language Impairments; Traumatic Brain Injury; Multiple Disabilities; Mental Retardation; Hearing Impairments; Gifted and Talented; Deafness/Blindness; Visual Impairments

Tactic Title:	**Monitoring On-Task Behavior**

Problem: Frequently, students have difficulty remaining on-task, and teacher time to monitor individual students is limited.

Tactic: First, establish a target behavior, such as staying in seat, writing, watching teacher, working with peer, etc. Then observe the student at the end of every 15-second interval for 10 minutes. At that exact second, note whether the student is on-task or off-task (see Momentary Time Sample Observation form that follows). The length of the interval must be equal across a single observation period; however, the length of the intervals can vary across lessons, depending on what you believe would provide the best information. If the student is off-task, describe the inappropriate behavior (talking out, head on desk, out of seat, etc.). Number of on-task behaviors ÷ number of observations × 100 = percentage of time on task.

For example: **O** = On-Task   **X** = Off-Task

X	X	X	O	O	O	X	O	O	O	O	X	X	O	O	O	X	O	O	O
X	X	X	O	O	O	O	X	X	X	O	O	O	X	O	O	O	X	O	O

On-Task:	25
Off-Task:	15
Total Observations:	40
Time On-Task:	$25 \div 40 \times 100 = 62.5\%$

Repeat a 10-minute observation at another time. Again, simply record whether the student is on- or off-task at the end of each 15-second interval. Calculate time on-task. Average the results from the two observation periods.

Example: I have used momentary time sampling to obtain some real data to help us know whether Samuel's in-seat behavior has improved. He is in a general education classroom for the first time this term, and that is our first step in helping him adjust to a classroom setting that is different from the Resource Room. I don't have time always to actually do the observations, so I ask my aide or the special education teacher to help out. He knows that we are observing his behavior; he wants to improve. He just isn't exactly sure when we're recording or for how long. Also, I would modify the sample so that I could note his behavior and what was happening at that time (lecture, small-group activity, discussion, etc.).

Philipa N., teacher

Benefits: Momentary time sampling

- provides specific data to aid in planning and modifying instruction;
- lets all those involved—teachers, parents, and the student—see what is actually happening;
- is applicable across a large number of observable behaviors; and
- can be conducted without disruption during class time.

Literature: Gunter, M. L., Venn, J. P., Miller, K. A., & Kelly, L. (2003). Efficacy of using momentary time samples to determine on-task behavior of students with emotional/behavioral disorders. *Education and Treatment of Children, 26*(4), 400–412.

Mars, H. van der (1994). Improving your instruction through self-evaluation: Part 5. Assessing student behaviors. *Strategies, 7*(6), 26–29.

Saudargas, R. A., & Zanolli, K. (1990). Momentary time sampling as an estimate of percentage time: A field violation. *Journal of Applied Behavior Analysis, 23*, 533–555.

Momentary Time Sample Observations

Student Name:_____   Date:_____ Class: _____

Times of Observation: _____

Observer: _____

Length of Observation: _____   # of Intervals:_____

Target Behavior: _____

	Classroom Activity	Student Behavior	On	Off
1				
2				
3				
4				
5				
6				
7				
8				
9				
10				
11				
12				
13				
14				
15				
16				
17				
18				
19				
20				
21				
22				
23				

	Classroom Activity	Student Behavior	On	Off
24				
25				
26				
27				
28				
29				
30				
31				
32				
33				
34				
35				
36				
37				
38				
39				
40				

Chapter 11: Monitor Engaged Time

Strategy:	**Teach Students to Monitor Their Own Participation**
Content Skills:	Mathematics/Problem Solving/Calculating; Reading; Social Studies; Science; Writing
Learning Difference:	Attention; Processing Visual Information; Self-Control; Processing Verbal Information; Cognition Low; Cognition Mixed; Memory Short-Term; Memory Long-Term; Study Skills; Processing Verbal Information; Receptive Language/Decoding (listening, reading); Expressive Language/Encoding (speaking, writing, spelling)
Disability Category:	Specific Learning Disabilities; Autism; Orthopedic or Other Health Impairments; Attention Deficit/Hyperactivity Disorder; Serious Emotional Disturbance; Speech or Language Impairments; Traumatic Brain Injury; Multiple Disabilities; Mental Retardation; Hearing Impairments; Gifted and Talented; Deafness/Blindness; Visual Impairments

Tactic Title:	**Self-Monitoring for On-Task Behavior**
Problem:	Frequently, students have difficulty remaining on-task and engage in behaviors that hinder their potential for learning.
Tactic:	First, prepare a tape or CD by recording a repeated tone or word, such as *check*. The intervals of repetition may vary according to the situation. The intervals may be set (e.g., every 30 seconds) or occur randomly (e.g., first after 10 seconds, then after 25 seconds, then after 90 seconds, etc.). Then give the student the Recording Worksheet. Set up the recording with headphones for the students. The student, upon hearing the prerecorded cue, places a checkmark in the column appropriate to his or her behavior at the time of the tone. Initially, students may need someone to oversee the procedure.
Example:	I've even used this tactic with an entire class, so we didn't need the headphones. I've found that as students become more familiarized with it, they learn to make automatic mental cues to monitor themselves. So I'm really teaching them a lifetime strategy! To encourage "honesty" in recording, sometimes I record simultaneously, and then we compare. Extra points for being in agreement with the teacher! *Jesse P., teacher*
Benefits:	Self-monitoring techniques • enable students to maintain their focus on classroom tasks and make the most of their learning time; • teach students to take greater responsibility for their learning;

- give teachers and students clear evidence of progress toward meeting goals/objectives; and
- are practical and effective.

Literature: Reid, R. (1996). Research in self-monitoring with students with learning disabilities: The present, the prospects, the pitfalls. *Journal of Learning Disabilities, 29*, 317–331.

Recording Worksheet

Student: _____ Date:_____ Time:_____

Target Behavior: _____

Directions: Turn on the recording. When you hear a tone, ask yourself whether you were _____. Then place a checkmark in the appropriate box in the Row #1. When you hear the tone again, ask the question again and place a checkmark in the appropriate box in Row #2. Continue until _____. Any questions?

	YES	NO
1		
2		
3		
4		
5		
6		
7		
8		
9		
10		
11		
12		
13		
14		
15		
16		
17		
18		
19		
20		
21		
22		
23		
24		

25		
26		
27		
28		
29		
30		
	Total:	**Total:**

12

Keep Records of
Student Progress

Principle	Strategy
Keep Records of Student Progress	Teach Students to Chart Their Own Progress
	Regularly Inform Students of Performance
	Maintain Records of Student Performance

Chapter 12: Keep Records of Student Progress

Strategy:	**Teach Students to Chart Their Own Progress**
Content Skills:	Writing; Science; Social Studies; Reading; Mathematics/Problem Solving/Calculating; Arts
Learning Difference:	Cognition Mixed; Expressive Language/Encoding (speaking, writing, spelling); Self-Confidence; Study Skills; Receptive Language/Decoding (listening, reading); Memory Long-Term; Cognition High; Cognition Low; Hearing; Health; Memory Short-Term; Seeing; Fine Motor (handwriting, articulation, etc.); Processing Visual Information; Processing Verbal Information
Disability Category:	Specific Learning Disabilities; Gifted and Talented; Visual Impairments; Deafness/Blindness; Hearing Impairments; Mental Retardation; Multiple Disabilities; Traumatic Brain Injury; Second Language Learning Needs; Serious Emotional Disturbance; Speech or Language Impairments; Attention Deficit/Hyperactivity Disorder; Orthopedic or Other Health Impairments; Autism

Tactic Title:	**Charting Achievements: Teaching Students to Self-Evaluate**
Problem:	Teachers often find that students are so focused on the day-to-day that they fail to see the bigger picture.
Tactic:	First, together with students, identify their targeted behaviors, skills, objectives, and/or goals. Focusing on one or two is fine. You might select weekly quiz scores, on-task behavior during a class period, meeting due dates, quality of compositions, etc. Use a line graph as follows: enter the time frame (class period, days, or weeks) on the horizontal axis. Enter the range of "scores" on the vertical axis. Enter the three most recent scores and draw a dotted vertical line. Calculate the mean for the three scores and place a red dot inside the baseline portion of the graph. The three most recent scores serve as baseline. Now mark the desired goal on the graph with a red star at some point in the future. Connect that point with the average baseline score with a red line. That line is called an "aimline"—the path that you and your student will try to meet or exceed. Whenever work is completed and scored, students enter their scores on their charts. Schedule times to meet with students regularly to review their charts and replan if necessary.
Example:	Charting scores has really gotten my biology students involved in their learning; they work very very hard to beat that "aimline." Whenever they record a score, they also write in their journals and reflect on the reasons for that score . . . why they did well, what they learned, what do they need to do to improve . . . etc. Once a week, we take about

15 minutes to share their charts with a peer, and I really try to review each chart at least every couple of days.

Lysita H., teacher

Benefits: Self-evaluation and charting

- enable students and teachers to pinpoint skills that need improvement and establish goals;
- motivate students to reach their goals and take greater responsibility for their learning; and
- enable students to see areas where they have improved over time and gain a sense of accomplishment.

Literature: Lee, D., & Gavine, D. (2003). Goal-setting and self-assessment in Year 7 students. *Educational Research, 45*(1), 49–59.

van Kraayenoord, C. E., & Paris, S. G. (1997). Australian students self-appraisal of their work samples and academic progress. *Elementary School Journal, 97*(5), 523–527.

Chapter 12: Keep Records of Student Progress

Strategy:	Regularly Inform Students of Performance
Content Skills:	Writing; Science; Social Studies; Reading; Mathematics/Problem Solving/Calculating; Arts
Learning Difference:	Cognition Mixed; Expressive Language/Encoding (speaking, writing, spelling); Self-Confidence; Study Skills; Receptive Language/Decoding (listening, reading); Memory Long-Term; Cognition High; Cognition Low; Hearing; Health; Memory Short-Term; Seeing; Fine Motor (handwriting, articulation, etc.); Processing Visual Information; Processing Verbal Information
Disability Category:	Specific Learning Disabilities; Gifted and Talented; Visual Impairments; Deafness/Blindness; Hearing Impairments; Mental Retardation; Multiple Disabilities; Traumatic Brain Injury; Second Language Learning Needs; Serious Emotional Disturbance; Speech or Language Impairments; Attention Deficit/Hyperactivity Disorder; Orthopedic or Other Health Impairments; Autism

Tactic Title:	Summarizing Student Performance
Problem:	Many students can become so overwhelmed by the amount of work and the expectations that they fail to take stock of their actual learning.
Tactic:	Use a Weekly Performance Summary to enable students to begin to think about their learning. Individual assignments can be entered and comments made in the appropriate box during the week. While symbols (checkmark, +, −, *) can be used, encourage students to make a few notes. At the end of the week, students review their work and summarize their achievements and/or reasons for not doing as well as they had planned. Meet with students regularly to review their summaries and plan for the future.
Example:	I keep summaries . . . for each student, and then we meet and compare our thinking. In this way, we are informing each other. . . . I learn a lot about their frustrations, their hopes, what they need . . . so I can be more effective as their teacher.
	Tito F., teacher
Benefits:	Using performance summaries

- teaches students to be more reflective and thoughtful about their learning;
- enables students to pinpoint reasons for succeeding and areas for improvement; and
- ensures that students and teachers are equally aware of student performance.

Literature: Stevens, D. D., & Levi, A. J. (2004). *Introduction to rubrics: An assessment tool to save grading time, convey effective feedback and promote student learning.* Sterling, VA: Stylus.

Twyman, T., & Tindal, G. (2007). Extending curriculum-based measurement into middle/secondary schools: The technical adequacy of the concept maze. *Journal of Applied School Psychology, 24*(1), 49–67.

Weekly Performance Summary

Assignment	Monday	Tuesday	Wednesday	Thursday	Friday	Summary
1.						
2.						
3.						
4.						
5.						
6.						
7.						

Chapter 12: Keep Records of Student Progress

Strategy:	**Maintain Records of Student Performance**

Content Skills: Fitness; Arts; Mathematics/Problem Solving/Calculating; Reading; Social Studies; Science; Writing

Learning Difference: Speaking/Talking; Attention; Processing Visual Information; Self-Control; Expressive Language/Encoding (speaking, writing, spelling); Fine Motor (handwriting, articulation, etc.); Processing Verbal Information; Social Behaviors; Self-Care; Cognition Mixed; Memory Short-Term; Memory Long-Term; Cognition High; Cognition Low; Mobility; Hearing; Health; Seeing; Study Skills; Gross Motor (running, walking, etc.); Receptive Language/Decoding (listening, reading); Social Knowledge; Self-Confidence

Disability Category: Autism; Orthopedic or Other Health Impairments; Attention Deficit/Hyperactivity Disorder; Speech or Language Impairments; Specific Learning Disabilities; Serious Emotional Disturbance; Second Language Learning Needs; Traumatic Brain Injury; Multiple Disabilities; Hearing Impairments; Mental Retardation; Gifted and Talented; Deafness/Blindness; Visual Impairments; Attention Deficit Disorder

Tactic Title:	**Keeping a Daily Record of Student Behavior**

Problem: It is typically difficult to measure the behavior and/or performance of a student with autism or other disabilities using traditional measures.

Tactic: First, make mental notes of the student's behavior and/or performance during each class period. Next, keep a journal where you can quickly jot down your thoughts about the student's behavior and/or performance after class. Some teachers develop a checklist with the student and the special education teacher to save time. Finally, meet with the special education teacher weekly to discuss each week's entries. During this meeting, discuss possible improvements that can be made for this student.

Example: I know it's important not only to monitor student performance but also to keep records. None of us has a lot of time. However, these records are invaluable when meeting with the student or special educators, or talking with parents. I just keep sticky notes with me at all times so that I can make a note before I forget. . . . Just a word or two triggers my recall when I'm making more formal notes at the end of class. I keep a notebook with separate sections for each student who needs careful documentation daily. . . . When I look back, I'm amazed at all the data; I never would be able to recall everything without the journal.

Lucy C., teacher

Benefits: Maintaining daily records of student behavior or learning

- provides evidence over time that can be used in planning;
- is a tool for discussion with students and parents regarding activities in the classroom; and
- reduces potential, unintentional sources of bias.

Literature: Jones, E. D., Wilson, R., & Bhojwani, S. (1997). Mathematics instruction for secondary students with learning disabilities. *Journal of Learning Disabilities, 30*(2), 151–163.

13

Use Data to Make Decisions

Principle	Strategy
Use Data to Make Decisions	Use Data to Decide if More Services Are Warranted
	Use Student Progress to Make Teaching Decisions
	Use Student Progress to Decide When to Discontinue Services

Chapter 13: Use Data to Make Decisions

Strategy:	**Use Data to Decide if More Services Are Warranted**

Content Skills:	Fitness; Arts; Mathematics/Problem Solving/Calculating; Reading; Social Studies; Science; Writing
Learning Difference:	Attention; Cognition High; Cognition Low; Mobility; Hearing; Seeing; Memory Long-Term; Memory Short-Term; Cognition Mixed; Health; Speaking/Talking; Study Skills; Fine Motor (handwriting, articulation, etc.); Gross Motor (running, walking, etc.); Processing Visual Information; Processing Verbal Information; Receptive Language/Decoding (listening, reading); Expressive Language/Encoding (speaking, writing, spelling); Social Knowledge; Self-Control; Social Behaviors; Self-Confidence; Self-Care
Disability Category:	Visual Impairments; Deafness/Blindness; Gifted and Talented; Hearing Impairments; Multiple Disabilities; Mental Retardation; Traumatic Brain Injury; Serious Emotional Disturbance; Specific Learning Disabilities; Speech or Language Impairments; Attention Deficit/Hyperactivity Disorder; Orthopedic or Other Health Impairments; Autism

Tactic Title:	**Modifying Grading Criteria According to Student Needs**

Problem:	Teachers often find that grading those with special needs and those without on exactly the same criteria/standards is not only inequitable but impossible.
Tactic:	First, to change grading criteria, collaborate with the special education teacher and the student to determine equitable modifications as to quantity and quality of, as well as timelines and due dates for work. Then decide how to weight the criteria of the grade. Next, decide if grading on the basis of improvement will benefit the student or not: Will the student be rewarded for improvement? Finally, have the student sign a contract agreeing to these terms. You might use the Grading Criteria form on page 163.
Example:	While policies dictate that I must follow certain rules and procedures, we do have some alternatives/allowances/latitude for my students with disabilities. This is only right, because while it has been said that *all* students will . . . , we know, in reality, that that is not possible. Students with disabilities have been given the opportunity to have an individual plan for their education that includes both instruction and evaluation. So I am not about to penalize my students by only providing one test score as the measure of their learning. So much more has been involved. . . . So I do what I can . . . modifying grading criteria, using pass/fail, portfolios (love them!), etc. Mostly, I just try to communicate with my students, their other teachers, the special educators, my administrators, their parents . . . anyone who

will listen: how hard they work; how much they have learned; and, most importantly, how accepted they are by everyone in our classroom. Bottom line: Having data that include assignments with modified grading criteria helps everyone at "IEP time" to decide if additional special education services are needed—or not.

Henry G., teacher

Benefits: Modifying grading criteria

- provides students with the promise of a fair and informative grading procedure;
- reduces student stress and enhances student motivation;
- provides teachers with additional information when making important decisions.

Literature: Bursuck, W. D., Munk, D. D., & Olson, M. M. (1999). The fairness of report card grading adaptations. *Remedial and Special Education, 20*(2), 84–90.

Grading Criteria

Date:	Goals/Objectives:	Date Met:	Comments:

Chapter 13: Use Data to Make Decisions

Strategy:	**Use Student Progress to Make Teaching Decisions**

Content Skills: Fitness; Arts; Mathematics/Problem Solving/Calculating; Reading; Social Studies; Science; Writing

Learning Difference: Attention; Cognition High; Cognition Low; Mobility; Hearing; Seeing; Memory Long-Term; Memory Short-Term; Cognition Mixed; Health; Speaking/Talking; Study Skills; Fine Motor (handwriting, articulation, etc.); Gross Motor (running, walking, etc.); Processing Visual Information; Processing Verbal Information; Receptive Language/ Decoding (listening, reading); Expressive Language/Encoding (speaking, writing, spelling); Social Knowledge; Self-Control; Social Behaviors; Self-Confidence; Self-Care

Disability Category: Visual Impairments; Deafness/Blindness; Gifted and Talented; Hearing Impairments; Multiple Disabilities; Mental Retardation; Traumatic Brain Injury; Serious Emotional Disturbance; Specific Learning Disabilities; Speech or Language Impairments; Attention Deficit/Hyperactivity Disorder; Orthopedic or Other Health Impairments; Autism

Tactic Title:	**Individualizing Assessment**

Problem: It can be challenging to find appropriate and informative assessment procedures for students with disabilities. However, we need to do so to make appropriate teaching decisions.

Tactic: First, when students with disabilities are placed in your classroom, collaborate with your special education teacher to obtain information about the types of disabilities involved, the individual instructional goals and objectives, each student's learning style, required and/ or recommended accommodations/modifications, whether assistive technology is needed, and resources that are available to you as the general education teacher. Ask for a copy or synopsis of the student's Individualized Educational Plan (IEP). Meet with the special education teacher to discuss different assessment tools/instruments that you can use to make informed instructional decisions. These may include a structured interview, a rating scales, simple observation, charting student performance, and portfolios in addition to the tools you use with all of your students. Finally, depending on your district/school policies, you may be able to use alternative grading criteria, such as pass/fail, for your students with disabilities.

Example: When I finally got my schedule and my class lists this fall, I realized that across my six class periods each day, I have 13 (out of 125) students with disabilities: 6 with learning disabilities, 2 with ADHD, 1 with autism, 1 with emotional disturbance, 1 with a hearing impairment, and 1 who is partially blind. I was about to learn about teaching diverse learners, for sure, and I needed help. First thing I did was to find their special education teachers, and I discovered that I was going to have a lot of support. The resource teacher would be in my classes ready to assist and coteach; teachers of the students with hearing and visual impairments would ensure that I had the equipment and modified materials I needed and also would be available to consult, demonstrate, and teach with me. Finally, I've found so many resources that are giving me background information on these different disability classifications. [See References and Additional Readings.] I'm learning all sorts of wonderful alternative ways to teach, and even better, my methods of assessing student progress now really give me the information I need to know what to do tomorrow. I may not be perfect at it yet, but it sure is a much more exciting way of teaching and I'm loving every minute of it.

Tyler T., teacher

Benefits: Aligning teaching and evaluation methods

- provides students with a clear and equitable method of assessment;
- gives teachers more accurate information for making instructional decisions; and
- increases the likelihood that students will be learning appropriate material and meeting the goals and objectives of their IEPs.

Literature: McKinney, J. D., Montague M., & Hocutt, A. M. (1993). Educational assessment of students with ADD. *Exceptional Children, 60,* 125–133.

Chapter 13: Use Data to Make Decisions

Strategy:	**Use Student Progress to Decide When to Discontinue Services**

Content Skills:	Fitness; Arts; Mathematics/Problem Solving/Calculating; Reading; Social Studies; Science; Writing
Learning Difference:	Attention; Cognition High; Cognition Low; Mobility; Hearing; Seeing; Memory Long-Term; Memory Short-Term; Cognition Mixed; Health; Speaking/Talking; Study Skills; Fine Motor (handwriting, articulation, etc.); Gross Motor (running, walking, etc.); Processing Visual Information; Processing Verbal Information; Receptive Language/Decoding (listening, reading); Expressive Language/Encoding (speaking, writing, spelling); Social Knowledge; Self-Control; Social Behaviors; Self-Confidence; Self-Care
Disability Category:	Visual Impairments; Deafness/Blindness; Gifted and Talented; Hearing Impairments; Multiple Disabilities; Mental Retardation; Traumatic Brain Injury; Serious Emotional Disturbance; Specific Learning Disabilities; Speech or Language Impairments; Attention Deficit/Hyperactivity Disorder; Orthopedic or Other Health Impairments; Autism

Tactic Title:	**Using Portfolios to Make Important Decisions**

Problem:	Most students who enter the special education "system" remain. Fewer than 5 percent leave. Accurate and informative assessment that includes both academic and social achievement information is essential in making decisions as to whether special education services are no longer needed.
Tactic:	Assessment tools and evaluation procedures should parallel successful instructional methods, including modifications and accommodations. In addition, accurate, ongoing data should be gathered over time from a multitude of sources and incorporated into the student's portfolio. Therefore, every teacher who is responsible for any aspect of a student's curriculum/program/schedule should provide data. These data might include, but are not limited to, tests and test scores, work samples, anecdotal records, logs of parent/teacher contacts and meetings with colleagues, video/audio tape recordings, CDs containing photographs of projects and presentations, student and teacher reflections, etc. The portfolio can provide the foundation for making accurate decisions regarding continuing or discontinuing special education services.
Example:	We've used student portfolios for several years in our own classrooms, so assembling one summative portfolio that includes data from every possible source really isn't that much extra work. Several of us in the math department have started keeping data electronically and submitting

it to the special education teacher periodically . . . so we don't have to push the panic button when IEP time rolls around. Several of my students with disabilities are really computer-literate, and they've started submitting the work electronically, which makes my job even easier.

Lisa T., teacher

Benefits: Using portfolios to make decisions

- provides a rich array of information from a variety of sources;
- enhances communication among parents, students, and professionals; and
- increases the likelihood that correct decisions are made.

Literature: Siegel-Causey, E., & Allinder, R. M. (1998). Using alternative assessment for students with severe disabilities: Alignment with best practices. *Educational Training in Mental Retardation and Developmental Disabilities, 33*(2), 168–178.

References

Algozzine, B., Campbell, P., & Wang, A. (2009). *63 Tactics for Teaching Diverse Learners: K–6*. Thousand Oaks, CA: Corwin.

Algozzine, B., & Ysseldyke, J. E. (1992). *Strategies and tactics for effective instruction*. Longmont, CO: Sopris West.

Algozzine, B., Ysseldyke, J. E., & Elliott, J. (1997). *Strategies and tactics for effective instruction* (2nd ed.). Longmont, CO: Sopris West.

Anhalt, K., McNeil, C. B., & Bahl, A. B. (1998). The ADHD classroom kit: A whole classroom approach for managing disruptive behavior. *Psychology in the Schools, 35*(1), 67–77.

Arntz, A. (1993). Treatment of borderline personality disorder: A challenge for cognitive-behavioral therapy. *Behavioral Research Therapy, 32*, 419–430.

Barkley, P. (1993). Eight principles to guide ADHD children. *The ADHD Report, 1*(2), 1–4.

Behrmann, M. M. (1995). *Assistive technology for students with mild disabilities* (ERIC Digest E529). Reston, VA: ERIC Clearinghouse on Disabilities and Gifted Education, Council for Exceptional Children. (ERIC Document Reproduction Service No. ED378755)

Behrmann, M. M., & Jerome, M. K. (2002). *Assistive technology for students with mild disabilities: Update 2002* (ERIC Digest E623). Arlington, VA: ERIC Clearinghouse on Disabilities and Gifted Education, Council for Exceptional Children. (ERIC Document Reproduction Service No. ED463595)

Beringer, V. W. (1997). Introduction to interventions for students with learning and behavior problems: Myths and realities. *School Psychology Review, 26*, 326–332.

Biddulph, G., Hess, P., & Humes, R. (2006). Helping a child with learning challenges be successful in the general education classroom. *Intervention in School & Clinic, 41*, 315–316.

Bloom, B. S. (1986). Automaticity: The hands and feet of genius. *Educational Leadership, 43*(5), 70–77.

Bottage, B. A. (1999). Effects of contextualized math instruction on problem solving on average and below-average achieving students. *Journal of Special Education, 33*, 81–92.

Bryan, T., & Sullivan-Burstein, K. (1998). From behavior to constructivism in teacher education. *Remedial and Special Education Journal, 19*, 263–275.

Bursuck, W. D., Munk, D. D., & Olson, M. M. (1999). The fairness of report card grading adaptations. *Remedial and Special Education, 20*(2), 84–90.

Camoni, G. A., & McGeehan, L. (1997). Peer buddies: A child-to-child support program. *Principal, 76*, 40–43.

Campbell, P., & Siperstein, G. (1994). *Improving social competence: A resource for elementary school teachers*. Boston: Allyn & Bacon.

Chandler, A. (1997). Is this for a grade? A personal look at journals. *English Journal, 86*, 45–49.

Chang, A. C.-S., & Read, J. (2008). Reducing listening test anxiety through various forms of listening support. *TESL-EJ, 12*(1), 1–25.

Dalton, B., Morocco, C., Tivnan, T., & Mead, P. R. (1997). Supported inquiry science: Teaching for conceptual change in urban and suburban science classrooms. *Journal of Learning Disabilities, 30*, 670–684.

Dollard, N. (1996). Constructive classroom management. *Focus on Exceptional Children, 29*, 1–12.

Drueke, J., & Streckfuss, R. (1996). Some first steps in teaching a strategy for fact finding. *Journalism and Mass Communication Educator, 51*(2), 5–79.

Dumas, M. C. (1998). The risk of social interaction: Problems among adolescents with ADHD. *Education and Treatment of Children, 21*, 447–460.

DuPaul, G. J., & Stoner, G. (1994). *ADHD in the schools: Assessment and intervention strategies.* New York: Guilford.

Epstein, T., & Elias, M. (1996). To reach for the stars: How social/affective education can foster truly inclusive environments. *Phi Delta Kappan, 78,* 157–163.

Farrel, M., & John, E. (1995). Literacy for all? The case of Down syndrome. *Journal of Reading, 38*(4), 270–280.

Ford, D. Y., & Harris III, J. J. (1999). *Multicultural gifted education.* New York: Teachers College Press.

Fowler, R. L. (1974). Effectiveness of highlighting for retention of text material. *Journal of Applied Psychology, 59,* 358–364.

Friend, M., & Bursuck, W. D. (2009). *Including students with special needs: A practical guide for teachers.* Boston: Allyn & Bacon.

Fuchs, L. S., & Fuchs, D. (1998). General educators' instructional adaptation for students with learning disabilities. *Learning Disability Quarterly, 21,* 23–33.

Graham, S., Schwartz, S., & MacArthur, C. (1993). Knowledge of writing and the composing process, attitude toward writing, and self-efficiency for students with and without learning disabilities. *Journal of Learning Disabilities, 26,* 237–249.

Griffin, L. L., & Butler, J. I. (Eds.). (2005). *Teaching games for understanding: Theory, research, and practice.* Champaign, IL: Human Kinetics.

Gunter, P. L., Denny, R. K., Jack, S. L., Shores, R. E., & Nelson, C. M. (1993). Aversive stimuli in academic interactions between students with serious emotional disturbance and their teachers. *Behavioral Disorders, 18*(4), 265–274.

Gunter, P. L., Venn, M. L., Patrick, J., Miller, K. A., & Kelly, L. (2003). Efficacy of using momentary time samples to determine on-task behavior of students with emotional/behavioral disorders. *Education and Treatment of Children, 26*(4), 400–412.

Henderson, H. A., & Fox, N. (1998). Inhibited and uninhibited children: Challenges in school settings. *School Psychology Review, 27,* 492–505.

Herbert, E., & Schultz, L. (1996). The power of portfolios. *Educational Leadership, 53*(7), 70–71.

Holzberg, C. S. (1995). Beyond the printed book. *Technology and Learning, 15,* 22–23.

Hurd, D. W. (1997). Novelty and its relation to field trips. *Education, 118,* 29–35.

Jackson, C. W., & Larkin, M. J. (2002). Rubrics: Teaching students to use grading rubrics. *Teaching Exceptional Children, 35*(1), 40–45.

Jones, E. D., Wilson, R., & Bhojwani, S. (1997). Mathematics instruction for secondary students with learning disabilities. *Journal of Learning Disabilities, 30*(2), 151–163.

Kohn, A. (1996). Beyond discipline. *Education Week, 16.* Retrieved November 11, 2008, from http://www.alfiekohn.org/teaching/edweek/discipline.htm

Lee, D., & Gavine, D. (2003). Goal-setting and self-assessment in Year 7 students. *Educational Research, 45*(1), 49–59.

Marjorie, M., & Applegate, B. (1993). Middle school students' mathematical problem solving: An analysis of think-aloud protocols. *Learning Disability Quarterly, 16,* 19–30.

Mars, H. van der. (1994). Improving your instruction through self-evaluation: Part 5. Assessing student behaviors. *Strategies, 7*(6), 26–29.

McKinney, J. D., Montague M., & Hocutt, A. M. (1993). Educational assessment of students with ADD. *Exceptional Children, 60,* 125–133.

Meeks, L. L. (1999). Making English classrooms happier places to learn. *English Journal, 88,* 73–79.

Metzler, C. W., Biglan, A., Rusby, J. C., & Sprague, J. R. (2001). Evaluation of a comprehensive behavior management program to improve school-wide positive behavior support. *Education & Treatment of Children, 24,* 448–480.

Moffatt, C. W., Hanley-Maxwell, C., & Donnellan, A. M. (1995). Discrimination of emotion, affective perspective taking and empathy in individuals with mental retardation. *Education and Training in Mental Retardation and Developmental Disabilities, 30,* 76–84.

Monberg, G. H., & Monberg, L. Z. (2006). Classrooms and teaching space. *School Planning & Management, 45*(2), 56–57.

Mulcahy, C. A. (2008). The effects of a contextualized instructional package on the area and perimeter performance of secondary students with emotional and behavioral disabilities (Doctoral dissertation, University of Maryland, 2007). *Dissertation Abstracts International, 68,* 8-A.

Nagel, P. (2008). Moving beyond lecture: Cooperative learning and the secondary social studies classroom. *Education, 128,* 363–368.

National Institute of Mental Health (NIMH). (2004). National Institute of Mental Health multimodal treatment study of ADHD follow-up: 24-month outcomes of treatment strategies for attention-deficit/hyperactivity disorder. *Pediatrics, 113,* 754–761.

Pearl, C. (2004). Laying the foundation for self-advocacy: Fourth graders with learning disabilities invite their peers into the resource room. *Teaching Exceptional Children, 36*(3), 44–49.

Reid, R. (1996). Research in self-monitoring with students with learning disabilities: The present, the prospects, the pitfalls. *Journal of Learning Disabilities, 29,* 317–331.

Reis, S. M., & Renzulli, J. S. (1992). Using curriculum compacting to challenge the above-average. *Educational Leadership, 50,* 51–57.

Renzulli, J. S., & Reis, S. M. (1998). Talent development through curriculum differentiation. *NASSP Bulletin, 82,* 61–74.

Richardson, J. S. (2000). *Read it aloud: Using literature in the secondary content classroom.* Newark, DE: International Reading Association.

Rose, T. D. (1999). Middle school teachers: Using individualized instruction strategies. *Intervention in School and Clinic, 34*(3), 137–142.

Saarimaki, P. (1995). Math in your world. *National Council of Teachers, 9,* 565–569.

Saudargas, R. A., & Zanolli, K. (1990). Momentary time sampling as an estimate of percentage time: A field violation. *Journal of Applied Behavior Analysis, 23,* 533–555.

Schneiderman, R. (with Werby, S.) (1996). *Homework improvement: A parent's guide to developing successful study habits in children before it's too late.* Tucson, AZ: Good Year Books.

Shafer, G. (1997). Reader response makes history. *English Journal, 86,* 65–68.

Shapiro, E. S., DuPaul, G. J., & Bradley-Klug, K. L. (1998). Self-management as a strategy to improve the classroom behavior of adolescents with ADHD. *Journal of Learning Disabilities, 31,* 545–555.

Shields, J., & Shealey, M. (1997). Educational computing gets powerful. *Technology and Learning, 18,* 20.

Shima, K., & Gsovski, B. K. (1996). Making a way for Diana. *Educational Leadership, 53*(5), 37–40.

Siegel-Causey, E., & Allinger, R. M. (1998). Using alternative assessment for students with severe disabilities: Alignment with best practices. *Education and Training in Mental Retardation and Developmental Disabilities, 33*(2), 168–175.

Soto, G. (2000). *Baseball in April and other stories* (10th anniversary ed.). New York: Harcourt.

Sprouse, C. A., Hall, C. W., Webster, R. E., & Bolen, L. M. (1998). Social perception in students with learning disabilities and attention deficit/hyperactivity disorder. *Journal of Nonverbal Behavior, 22,* 125–134.

Stenhoff, D. M., & Lignugaris, B. (2007). A review of the effects of peer tutoring on students with mild disabilities in secondary settings. *Exceptional Children, 74,* 8–30.

Stevens, D. D., & Levi, A. J. (2004). *Introduction to rubrics: An assessment tool to save grading time, convey effective feedback and promote student learning.* Sterling, VA: Stylus.

Stormont-Spurgin, M. (1997). I lost my homework: Strategies for improving organization in students with ADHD. *Intervention in School and Clinic, 32,* 270–274.

Tinzmann, M. B., Jones, B. F., Fennimore, T. F., Bakker, C. F., & Pierce, J. (1990). *What is the collaborative classroom?* Oak Brook, IL: North Central Regional Educational Laboratory (NCREL).

Twyman, T., & Tindal, G. (2007). Extending curriculum-based measurement into middle/secondary schools: The technical adequacy of the concept maze. *Journal of Applied School Psychology, 24*(1), 49–67.

van Kraayenoord, C. E., & Paris, S. G. (1997). Australian students' self-appraisal of their work samples and academic progress. *Elementary School Journal, 97*(5), 523–537.

Ward-Lonergan, J. M., Liles, B. Z., & Owen, S. V. (1996). Contextual strategy instruction: Socially/emotionally maladjusted adolescents with language impairments. *Journal of Communication Disorders, 29,* 107–124.

Webb-Johnson, G., Artiles, A. J., Trent, S. C., Jackson, C. W., & Velox, A. (1998). The status of research on multicultural education in teacher education and special education: Problems, pitfalls and promises. *Remedial and Special Education, 19*(1), 7–15.

Zahorik, J. A. (1999). Reducing class size leads to individualized instruction. *Educational Leadership, 57*(1), 50–53.

Additional Readings

Abbott, M., Walton, C., & Greenwood, C. R. (2002). Phonemic awareness in kindergarten and first grade. *Teaching Exceptional Children, 34*(4), 20–26.

Aber, M. E., Bachman, B., Campbell, P., & O'Malley, G. (1994). Improving instruction in elementary schools. *Teaching Exceptional Children, 26*(3), 42–50.

Allsopp, D. H. (1997). Using classwide peer tutoring to teach beginning algebra problem-solving skills in heterogeneous classrooms. *Remedial and Special Education, 18,* 367–379.

AlphaSmart Direct Inc. (2008). *AlphaSmart™.* Retrieved November 11, 2008, from http://www.alphasmart.com

Anderson, L. W., & Krathwohl, D. R. (Eds.). (2001). *A taxonomy for learning, teaching, and assessing: A revision of Bloom's taxonomy of educational objectives* (abridged ed.). New York: Longman.

Armstrong, D. C. (1994). Gifted child's education requires real dialogue: The use of interactive writing for collaborative education. *Gifted Child Quarterly, 38,* 136–145.

Arreaga-Mayer, C. (1998). Increasing active student responding and improving academic performance through class-wide peer tutoring. *Intervention in School and Clinic, 34,* 89–94.

Batshaw, M. L. (Ed.). (1997). *Children with disabilities* (4th ed.). Baltimore: Brookes.

Batshaw, M. L., Pellegrino, L., & Roizen, N. J. (Eds.). (2007). *Children with disabilities* (6th ed.). Baltimore: Brookes.

Behrmann, M. M. (1994). Assistive technology for students with mild disabilities. *Intervention in School and clinic, 30*(2), 70–82.

Beirne-Smith, M. (1991). Peer tutoring in arithmetic for children with learning disabilities. *Exceptional Children, 57*(4), 330–337.

Belfiore, P. J., Grskovic, J. A., Murphy, A. M., & Zentall, S. S. (1996). The effects of antecedent color on reading for students with learning disabilities and co-occurring attention-deficit/hyperactivity disorder. *Journal of Learning Disabilities, 29,* 432–438.

Bergman, A. B. (1993). Performance assessment for early childhood. *Science and Children, 30*(5), 20–22.

Bernstorf, E. D., & Welsbacher, B. T. (1996). Helping students in the inclusive classroom. *Music Educators Journal, 82,* 21–37.

Birenbaum, M., & Feldman, R. A. (1998).Relationships between learning patterns and attitudes toward two assessment formats. *Educational Research, 40,* 90.

Bolocofsky, D. N. (1980). Motivational effects of classroom competition as a function of field dependence. *Journal of Educational Research, 73,* 213–217.

Bonus, M., & Riordan, L. (1998). *Increasing student on-task behavior through the use of specific seating arrangements* (Master's Action Research Project). Chicago: Saint Xavier University. (ERIC Document Reproduction Service No. ED422129)

Bos, C. S., Mather, N., Silver-Pacuilla, H., & Narr, R. F. (2000). Learning to teach early literacy skills collaboratively. *Teaching Exceptional Children, 32*(5), 38–45.

Boulineau, T., Fore III, C., Hagan-Burke, S., & Burke, M. D. (2004). Use of story-mapping to increase the story-grammar text comprehension of elementary students with learning disabilities. *Learning Disability Quarterly, 27,* 105–120.

Bower, B. (1989). Remodeling the autistic child. *Science News, 136,* 312–313.

Bromley, K., & Mannix, D. (1993). Beyond the classroom: Publishing student work in magazines. *Reading Teacher, 47,* 72–77.

Browder, D. M., Wakeman, S. Y., Spooner, F., Ahlgrim-Delzell, L., & Algozzine, B. (2006). Research on reading instruction for individuals with significant cognitive disabilities. *Exceptional Children, 72,* 392–408.

Brulle, C. G. (1994). Elementary school student responses to teacher directions. *Education and Treatment of Children, 17,* 459–467.

Bryant, P. E., Bradley, L., & Maclean, M. (1989). Nursery rhymes, phonological skills, and reading. *Journal of Child Language, 16,* 407–428.

Burns, B. (2006). *How to teach balanced reading and writing* (2nd ed.). Thousand Oaks, CA: Corwin.

Burns, M. S., Delclos, V. R., & Kulewicz, S. J. (1987). Effects of dynamic assessment on teachers expectations of handicapped children. *American Educational Research Journal, 24,* 325–336.

Bursuck, W., Polloway, E. A., Plante, L., Epstein, M. H., Jayanthi, M., & McConeghy, J. (1996). Report card grading and adaptations: A national survey of classroom practices. *Exceptional Children, 62,* 301–305.

Burton, A. W., & Rodgerson, R. W. (2001). New perspectives on the assessment of movement skills and motor abilities. *Adapted Physical Activity Quarterly, 18,* 347–365.

Campbell, P. S., & Scott-Kassner, C. (1995). *Music in childhood: From preschool through the elementary grades.* New York: Schirmer.

Case-Smith, J. (1996). Half-pint smarts. *American Journal of Occupational Therapy, 49,* 39–40.

Cavalier, A., Ferretti, R. P., Hodges, A. E., Cavalier, A., Ferretti, R. P., & Hodges, A. E. (1997). Self-management within a classroom token economy for students with learning disabilities. *Research in Developmental Disabilities, 18,* 167–178.

Charney, R. S. (2002). *Teaching children to care: Classroom management for ethical and academic growth, K–8* (rev. ed.). Turners Falls, MA: Northeast Foundation for Children.

Chesapeake Institute & Widmeyer Group. (1994). *101 ways to help children with ADD learn: Tips from successful teachers.* Washington, DC: Division of Innovation and Development, Office of Special Education Programs, Office of Special Education and Rehabilitative Services, U.S. Department of Education (ERIC Document Reproduction Service No. ED389109)

Chesapeake Institute. (1994). *Attention deficit disorder: What teachers should know.* Washington, DC: Division of Innovation and Development Office of Special Education Programs, Office of Special Education and Rehabilitative Services, U.S. Department of Education. (ERIC Document Reproduction Service No. ED370336)

Clarke-Klein, S. M. (1994). Expressive phonological deficiencies: Impact on spelling development. *Topics in Language Disorders, 14,* 40.

Cohen, M. (1993). Machines for thinking: The computer's role in schools. *Educational and Training Technology International, 30,* 57.

Cornoldi, C., Rigoni, F., Thessoldi, P. E., & Vio, C. (1999). Imagery deficits in nonverbal learning disabilities. *Journal of Learning Disabilities, 32,* 48–58.

Corral, N., & Antia, S. D. (1997). Self-talk: Strategies for success in math. *Teaching Exceptional Children, 29,* 42–45.

Coyne, M. D., Sipoli, R. P., & Ruby, M. F. (2006). Beginning reading instruction for students at risk for reading disabilities: What, how, and when. *Intervention in School and Clinic, 41,* 161–168.

Crozier, S., & Tincani, M. J. (2005). Using a modified social story to decrease disruptive behavior of a child with autism. *Focus on Autism and Other Developmental Disabilities, 20,* 150–157.

Cunningham, P. (1998). How tutoring works. *Instructor, 107,* 36.

Daniels, H., Zemelman, S., & Bizar, M. (1999). Whole language works: Sixty years of research. *Educational Leadership, 57*(2), 32–36.

del'Etoile, S. (1996). Meeting the needs of the special learner in music. *American Music Teacher, 45,* 10–13.

de la Paz, S., & Graham, S. (1997). Strategy instruction in planning: Effects on the writing performance and behavior of students. *Exceptional Children, 63,* 167–181.

Desrochers, J. (1999). Vision problems: How teachers can help. *Young Children, 54*(2), 36–38.

Dockrell, J. E., Lindsay, G., Connelly, V., & Mackie, C. (2007). Constraints in the production of written text in children with specific language impairments. *Exceptional Children, 73,* 147–164.

Dollard, N., & Christensen, L. (1996). Constructive classroom management. *Focus on Exceptional Children, 29*, 1–11.

Dowd, J. (1997). Refusing to play the blame game. *Educational Leadership, 54*, 67–69.

Duffy-Hester, A. (1999). Teaching struggling readers in elementary school classrooms: A review of classroom reading programs and principles for instruction. *The Reading Teacher, 52*, 480–495.

Dunton, J. (1998). The four Bs of classroom management. *Techniques: Making Education and Career Connections, 73*, 32–33.

Eakin, S., & Douglas, V. (1971). Automatization and oral reading problems in children. *Journal of Learning Disabilities, 4*, 31–38.

Eastman, B. G., & Rasbury, W. C. (1981). Cognitive self-instruction for the control of impulsive classroom behavior: Ensuring the treatment package. *Journal of Abnormal Child Psychology, 93*, 381–387.

Educational Resources Information Center. (1998). *Teaching children with attention deficit/hyperactivity disorder.* Reston, VA: ERIC Clearinghouse on Disabilities and Gifted Education, Council for Exceptional Children. (ERIC Document Reproduction Service No. ED423633)

Edyburn, D. L. (2000). Assistive technology and students with mild disabilities. *Focus on Exceptional Children, 32*(9), 1–22.

Elksnin, L. (1997). Collaborative speech and language services for students with learning disabilities. *The Journal of Learning Disabilities, 30*, 414–426.

Enright, D. S., & Gomez, B. (1985). PRO-ACT: Six strategies for organizing peer interaction in elementary classrooms. *The Journal for the National Association for Bilingual Education, 9*(3), 5–24.

Epstein, M., Polloway, E., Buck, G., Bursuck, W., Wissinger, L., Whitehouse, F., et al. (1997). Homework-related communication problems: Perspectives of general education teachers. *Learning Disabilities Research and Practice, 12*, 221–227.

Erdmann, L. (1994). *Success at last.* Portsmouth, NH: Heinemann.

Fachin, K. (1996). Teaching Tommy: A second-grader with attention deficit hyperactivity disorder. *Phi Delta Kappan, 77*, 437–442.

Farrow, L. (1996). A quartet of success stories: How to make inclusion work. *Educational Leadership, 53*(5), 51–55.

Fleischner, J. E., & Manheimer, M. A. (1997). Math interventions for students with learning disabilities: Myths and realities. *School Psychology Review, 26*, 397–413.

Forgan, J. W., & Gonzales-DeHass, A. (2004). How to infuse social skills training into literacy instruction. *Teaching Exceptional Children, 36*(6), 24–30.

Friar, K. K. (1999). Changing voices, changing times. *Music Educators Journal, 86*(3), 26–29.

Friedland, E. S., & Truesdell, K. S. (2006). "I can read to whoever wants to hear me read": Buddy readers speak out with confidence. *Teaching Exceptional Children, 38*(5), 36–42.

Fuchs, D., Fuchs, L. S., & Compton, D. L. (2004). Identifying reading disabilities by responsiveness to instruction: Specifying measures and criteria. *Learning Disability Quarterly, 27*, 216–228.

Fuchs, D., Fuchs, L. S., McMaster, K. L., Yen, L., & Svenson, E. (2004). Nonresponders: How to find them? How to help them? What do they mean for special education? *Teaching Exceptional Children, 37*(1), 72–77.

Fuchs, D., Fuchs, L. S., Thompson, A., Al Otaiba, S., Yen, L., Yang, N. J., et al. (2002). Exploring the importance of reading programs for kindergartners with disabilities in mainstream classrooms. *Exceptional Children, 68*, 295–311.

Fuchs, L. S., Compton, D. L., Fuchs, D., Paulsen, K., Bryant, J., & Hamlett, C. L. (2005). Responsiveness to intervention: Preventing and identifying mathematics disability. *Teaching Exceptional Children, 37*(4), 60–63.

Fuchs, L. S., Fuchs, D., & Compton, D. L. (2004). Monitoring early reading development in first grade: Word identification fluency versus nonsense word fluency. *Exceptional Children, 71*, 7–21.

Fuchs, L. S., Fuchs, D., Hamlett, C. L., Hope, S. K., Hollenbeck, K. N., Capizzi, A. M., et al. (2006). Extending responsiveness-to-intervention to math problem solving at third grade. *Teaching Exceptional Children, 38*(4), 59–63.

Fuchs, L. S., Fuchs, D., Prentice, K., Burch, M., & Paulsen, K. (2002). Hot math: Promoting mathematical problem solving among third-grade students with disabilities. *Teaching Exceptional Children, 35*(1), 70–73.

Fulk, B. M., Lohman, D., & Belfiore, P. J. (1997). Effects of integrated picture mnemonics on the letter recognition and letter-sound acquisition of transitional first-grade students with special needs. *Learning Disability Quarterly, 20,* 33–42.

Gallas, K. (1991). Arts as epistemology: Enabling children to know what they know. *Harvard Educational Review, 61,* 93–105.

Garcia, T. (2007). Facilitating the reading process. *Teaching Exceptional Children, 39*(3), 12–17.

Gardill, M. C., DuPaul, G. J., & Kyle, K. E. (1996). Classroom strategies for managing students with attention-deficit/hyperactivity disorder. *Intervention in School and Clinic, 32,* 89–94.

Gately, S. E. (2004). Developing concept of word: The work of emergent readers. *Teaching Exceptional Children, 36*(6), 16–22.

Geocaris, C., & Ross, M. (1999). A test worth taking. *Educational Leadership, 57*(1), 29–33.

Gerber, A., & Klein, E. R. (2004). A speech-language approach to early reading success. *Teaching Exceptional Children, 36*(6), 8–14.

Getch, Y., Bhukhanwala, F., & Neuharth-Pritchett, S. (2007). Strategies for helping children with diabetes in elementary and middle schools. *Teaching Exceptional Children, 39*(3), 46–51.

Gfeller, K. (1989). Behavior disorders: Strategies for the music teacher. *Music Educators Journal, 7,* 27–30.

Ghaziuddin, M., Leininger, L., & Tsai, L. (1995). Brief report: Thought disorder in Asperger syndrome; Comparison with high-functioning autism. *Journal of Autism and Developmental Disorders, 25,* 311–317.

Gibson, D., Haeberli, F. B., & Glover, T. A. (2005). Use of recommended and provided testing accommodations. *Assessment for Effective Intervention, 31,* 19–36.

Giordano, G. (1984). Analyzing and remediating writing disabilities. *Journal of Learning Disabilities, 17,* 78–83.

Glazer, S. M. (1998). Encouraging remarks. *Teaching PreK–8, 29,* 124–126.

Goolsby, T. W. (1999). Assessment in instrumental music. *Music Educators Journal, 95,* 31.

Graham, S., & Harris, K. R. (2006). Preventing writing difficulties: Providing additional handwriting and spelling instruction to at-risk children in first grade. *Teaching Exceptional Children, 38*(5), 64–66.

Graves, M., & Graves, B. (1996). Scaffolding reading experiences for inclusive classes. *Educational Leadership, 53*(5), 14–16.

Hankins, K. H. (1998). Cacophony to symphony: Memoirs in teacher research. *Harvard Educational Review, 68*(1), 80–95.

Harris, K. C., & Nevin, A. (1994). Developing and using collaborative bilingual special education teams. In L. M. Malave (Ed.), *Annual Conference Journal, NABE '92–'93* (pp. 25–35). Washington, DC: National Association for Bilingual Education. (ERIC Document Reproduction Service No. ED372643)

Hebert, E. A. (1998). Lessons learned about student portfolios. *Phi Delta Kappan, 80,* 583–585.

Hernandez, H. (1997). *Teaching in multicultural classrooms: A teacher's guide to context, process, and content.* New York: Simon and Schuster.

Higdon, H. (1999). Getting their attention. *Runner's World, 34,* 84.

Higgins, E. L., & Raskind, M. H. (1995). Compensatory effectiveness of speech recognition on the written composition performance of post-secondary students with learning disabilities. *Learning Disabilities Quarterly, 18,* 159–174.

Hitchcock, C. H., Prater, M. A., & Dowrick, P. W. (2004). Reading comprehension and fluency: Examining the effects of tutoring and video self-modeling on first-grade students with reading difficulties. *Learning Disability Quarterly, 27,* 89–103.

How to manage your students with ADD/ADHD. (1997). *Instructor, 106*(6), 63–65.

Huang, A., Mellblom, C., & Pearman, E. (1997). Inclusion of all students: Concerns and incentives of educators. *Education and Training in Mental Retardation and Developmental Disabilities, 32,* 11–20.

Huber, J. (1997). Laptop word processor: A way to close the technology gap. *Technology Connection, 4*(2), 26–28.

Hudson, P. (1997). Using teacher-guided practice to help students with learning disabilities acquire and retain social studies content. *Learning Disability Quarterly, 20,* 23–32.

Humpal, M. E., & Dimmick, J. A. (1995). Special learners in the music classroom. *Music Educators Journal, 81,* 21–23.

James, L. A., Abbot, M., & Greenwood, C. R. (2001). How Adam became a writer: Winning writing strategies for low-achieving students. *Teaching Exceptional Children, 33*(3), 30–37.

Jitendra, A. K. (2002). Teaching students math problem resolving through graphic representations. *Teaching Exceptional Children, 34*(4), 34–38.

Jitendra, A. K., Rohena-Diaz, E., & Nolet, V. (1998). A dynamic curriculum-based language assessment. *Preventing School Failure, 42,* 182–185.

Johnson, D. (1990). Why can't my student learn like everyone else? *Adult Learning, 2*(2), 24–25, 28.

Johnson, G. M. (1999). Inclusive education: Fundamental instructional strategies and considerations. *Preventing School Failure, 43,* 72.

Johnson, K. K. (1998). Teaching Shakespeare to learning disabled students. *English Journal, 83,* 45.

Johnson, L., Graham, S., & Harris, K. R. (1997). The effects of goal setting and self-instruction on learning a reading comprehension strategy: A study of students with learning disabilities. *Journal of Learning Disabilities, 30,* 80–91.

Justice, L. M., & Kaderavek, J. (2002). Using shared storybook reading to promote emergent literacy. *Teaching Exceptional Children, 34*(4), 8–13.

Kameenui, E. J., & Carnine, D. W. (1998). *Effective strategies that accommodate diverse learners.* Columbus, OH: Merrill/Prentice Hall.

Kemp, S., Fister, S., & McLaughlin, P. J. (1995). Academic strategies for children with ADD. *Intervention in School and Clinic, 30,* 203–210.

Kleinert, H. L., Kennedy, S., & Kearns, J. F. (1999). The impact of alternate assessments: A statewide teacher survey. *The Journal of Special Education, 33,* 93–102.

Korinek, L. (1993). Positive behavior management: Fostering responsible student behavior. In B. S. Billingsley (with D. Peterson, D. Bodkins, & M. B. Hendricks, Eds.), *Program leadership for serving students with disabilities* (pp. 263–298). Blacksburg and Richmond: Virginia Polytechnic Institute and State University and Virginia State Department of Education. (ERIC Document Reproduction Service No. ED372537)

Kowalski, E., Lieberman, L., Pucci, G., & Mulawka, C. (2005). Implementing IEP or 504 goals and objectives into general physical education. *The Journal of Physical Education, Recreation, & Dance, 76*(7), 33–37.

Kroeger, S. D., & Kouche, B. (2006). Using peer-assisted learning strategies to increase response to intervention in inclusive middle math settings. *Teaching Exceptional Children, 38*(5), 6–13.

Lambie, R. A. (1986). Adaptations for written expression. *Academic Therapy, 22,* 27–34.

Lane, K. L., Graham, S., Harris, K. R., & Weisenbach, J. L. (2006). Teaching writing strategies to young students struggling with writing and at risk for behavioral disorders: Self-regulated strategy development. *Teaching Exceptional Children, 39*(1), 60–64.

Lee, Y. J. (2006). The process-oriented ESL writing assessment: Promises and challenges. *Journal of Second Language Writing, 15,* 307–330.

Levy, N. R. (1996). Classroom strategies for managing students with attention-deficit/hyperactivity disorder. *Intervention in School and Clinic, 32*(2), 89–94.

Lewis, M., Wray, D., & Rospigliosi, P. (1994). Making reading for information more accessible to children with learning difficulties. *Support for Learning, 9,* 155–161.

Lewis, R. B. (1998). Assistive technology and learning disabilities: Today's realities and tomorrow's promises. *Journal of Learning Disabilities, 31,* 16–26.

Logan, K. R. (1998). Comparing instructional contexts of students with and without severe disabilities in general education classrooms. *Exceptional Children, 64,* 343–358.

Lombardi, T., & Butera, G. (1998). Mnemonics: Strengthening thinking skills of students with special needs. *The Clearing House, 71,* 284–287.

MacArthur, C., Graham, S., & Schwartz, S. (1995). Evaluation of a writing instruction model that integrated a process approach, strategy instruction, and word processing. *Learning Disability Quarterly, 18,* 278–294.

Macy, M. G., & Bricker, D. D. (2007). Embedding individualized social goals into routine activities in inclusive early childhood classrooms. *Early Child Development & Care, 177,* 107–120.

Majsterek, D. J. (1990). Writing disabilities: Is word processing the answer? *Intervention in School and Clinic, 26*(2), 93–97.

Malloy, W. (1997). Responsible inclusion: Celebrating diversity and academic excellence. *NASSP Bulletin, 81,* 80–85.

Manzo, A. V., Manzo, U. C., & Thomas, M. M. (2006). Rationale for systematic vocabulary development: Antidote for state mandates. *Journal of Adolescent & Adult Literacy, 49,* 610–619.

Marek-Schroer, M. F., & Schroer, N. A. (1993). Identifying and providing for musically gifted young children. *Roeper Review, 16*(1), 33–36.

Martens, P. (1998). Using retrospective miscue analysis to inquire: Learning from Michael. *The Reading Teacher, 52,* 176–180.

Martinez-Roldan, C. M., & Lopez-Robertson, J. M. (2000). Initiating literature circles in a first grade bilingual classroom. *The Reading Teacher, 53,* 270–281.

Marzano, R. J., Pickering, D. J., & Pollack, J. E. (2003). *Classroom instruction that works: Research based strategies for increasing student achievement.* Alexandria, VA: Association for Supervision and Curriculum Development.

Mastropieri, M. A., & Scruggs, T. E. (1997). Best practices in promoting reading comprehension in students with learning disabilities. *Remedial and Special Education, 18,* 197–213.

Mayer, G. R. (1999). Constructive discipline for school personnel. *Education and Treatment of Children, 22,* 36–54.

McEwan, E. K. (1998). *The ADHD intervention checklist.* Thousand Oaks, CA: Corwin.

McGrail, L. (1998). Modifying regular classroom curricula for high ability students. *Gifted Child Today, 21*(2), 36–39.

McLoughlin, J. A., & Lewis, R. B. (1994). *Assessing special students.* New York: Macmillan.

McNaughton, D. (1994). Spelling instruction for students with learning disabilities: Implications for research and practice. *Learning Disability Quarterly, 17,* 169–185.

McReynolds, J. C. (1988). Helping visually impaired students succeed in band. *Music Educators Journal, 71,* 35–38.

Meisels, S. J. (1997).Using work sampling in authentic assessments. *Educational Leadership, 54*(4), 60–65.

Michaels, C. A., Brown, F., & Mirabella, N. (2005). Personal paradigm shifts in PBS experts: Perceptions of treatment acceptability of decelerative consequence-based behavioral procedures. *Journal of Positive Behavioral Supports, 7,* 93–108.

Miller, S. P., & Hudson, P. J. (2006). Helping students with disabilities understand what mathematics means. *Teaching Exceptional Children, 39*(1), 28–35.

Montali, J., & Lewandowski, L. (1996). Bimodal reading: Benefits of a talking computer for average and less skilled readers. *Journal of Learning Disabilities, 29,* 271–279.

Montello, L., & Coons, E. E. (1998). Effects of active versus passive group music therapy on preadolescents with emotional, learning, and behavioral disorders. *Journal of Music Therapy, 35*(1), 49–67.

Monty, N. D. (1997). Transforming student assessment. *Phi Delta Kappan, 79,* 30–40, 58.

Moore, A. (1996). Assessing young readers: Questions of culture and ability. *Language Arts, 73,* 306–316.

Moran, M. R. (1987). Individualized objectives for writing instruction. *Topics in Language Disorders, 7,* 42–54.

Morgan, M., & Moni, K. B. (2005). Use phonics activities to motivate learners with difficulties. *Intervention in School and Clinic, 41*(1), 42–45.

Morgan, M., & Moni, K. B. (2007). Motivate students with disabilities using sight-vocabulary activities. *Intervention in School & Clinic, 48,* 229–233.

Morgan, P. L., & Fuchs, D. (2007). Is there a bidirectional relationship between children's reading skills and reading motivation? *Exceptional Children, 73,* 165–183.

Moxley, R. A. (1998). Treatment-only designs and student self-recording as strategies for public school teachers. *Education and Treatment of Children, 21*(1), 37–61.

Munk, D. D., & Bursuck, W. D. (1998). Can grades be helpful and fair? *Educational Leadership, 55,* 44.

Murphy, D. M. (1996). Implications of inclusion for general and special education. *The Elementary School Journal, 96,* 469–493.

National Board for Professional Teaching Standards. (2008). *The standards.* Retrieved November 11, 2008, from http://www.nbpts.org/the_standards/

National Joint Committee on Learning Disabilities. (1993). Providing appropriate education for students with learning disabilities in regular education classrooms. *Journal of Learning Disabilities, 26,* 330–332.

Newman, J. (1998). *Tensions of teaching: Beyond tips to critical reflection.* New York: Teachers College Press.

Niebling, B. C., & Elliott, S. N. (2005). Testing accommodations and inclusive assessment practices. *Assessment for Effective Intervention, 31*(1), 1–6.

Novelli, J. (1997). Seating solutions. *Primary Instructor, 107*(2), 78–79.

Olinghouse, N. G., Lambert, W., & Compton, D. L. (2006). Monitoring children with reading disabilities' response to phonics intervention: Are there differences between intervention-aligned and general skill progress monitoring assessments? *Exceptional Children, 73*, 90–106.

Ormond, J. E. (1998). *Educational psychology: Developing learners* (2nd ed.). Upper Saddle River, NJ: Prentice Hall.

Ortiz, A. A. (1997). Learning disabilities occurring concomitantly with linguistic differences. *Journal of Learning Disabilities, 30*, 321–332.

Patzer, C. E., & Pettegrew, B. S. (1996). Finding a voice: Primary students with developmental disabilities express personal meanings through writing. *Teaching Exceptional Children, 29*(2), 22–27.

Perry, L. A. (1997). Using wordless picture books with beginning readers (of any age). *Teaching Exceptional Children, 29*(3), 68–69.

Pfiffner, L. J. (1998). *All about ADHD: The complete practical guide for classroom teachers.* New York: Scholastic Books.

Prater, M. A. (1992). Increasing time-on-task in the classroom. *Intervention in School and Clinic, 28*(1), 22–27.

Quinn, M. M., Gable, R. A., Rutherford, R. B., Nelson, C. M., & Howell, K. W. (1998). *Addressing student problem behavior: An IEP team's introduction to functional behavior assessment and behavior intervention plans* (2nd ed.). Washington, DC: American Institute for Research: Center for Effective Collaboration and Practice.

Raver, S. A. (2004). Monitoring child progress in early childhood special education settings. *Teaching Exceptional Children, 36*(6), 52–57.

Reason, R. (1999). ADHD: A psychological response to an evolving concept. *Journal of Learning Disabilities, 32*, 85–91.

Reis, S. M., Burns, D. E., & Renzulli, J. S. (1995). *Curriculum compacting: The complete guide to modifying the regular curriculum for high ability students.* Mansfield Center, CT: Creative Learning Press.

Rhizzo, T., Faison-Hodge, J., Woodard, R., & Sayers, K. (2003). Factors affecting social experiences in inclusive physical education. *Adapted Physical Activity Quarterly, 20*(3), 317.

Riccomini, P. J. (2005). Identification and remediation of systematic error patterns in subtraction. *Learning Disability Quarterly, 28*, 233–242.

Richardson, C. (1990). Measuring musical giftedness. *Music Education Journal, 76*, 40.

Riley, G., Beard, L. A., & Strain, J. (2004). Assistive technology at use in the teacher education programs at Jacksonville State University. *TechTrends: Linking Research & Practice to Improve Learning, 48*(6), 47–49.

Ritchey, K. D. (2006). Learning to write: Progress-monitoring tolls for beginning and at-risk writers. *Teaching Exceptional Children, 39*(2), 22–26.

Roberson, T. (1984). Determining curriculum content for the gifted. *Roeper Review, 6*, 137–139.

Robinson, M. (1995). Alternative assessment techniques for teachers. *Music Educators Journal, 81*, 28–34.

Rock, E. E., Fessler, M. A., & Church, R. P. (1997). The concomitance of learning disabilities and emotional/behavioral disorders: A conceptual model. *Journal of Learning Disabilities, 30*, 245–260.

Rodriguez, D., Parmar, R. S., & Signer, B. R. (2001). Fourth-grade culturally and linguistically diverse exceptional students' concepts of number line. *Exceptional Children, 67*, 199–210.

Rosner, J. (1993). *Helping children overcome learning difficulties* (3rd ed.). New York: Walker.

Ruth, W. J. (1996). Goal setting and behavior contracting for students with emotional and behavioral difficulties. *Psychology in the Schools, 33*, 153–158.

Ryba, K., Selby, L., & Nolan, P. (1995). Computers empower students with special needs. *Educational Leadership, 53*, 82–84.

Saddler, B., & Preschern, J. (2007). Improving sentence-writing ability through sentence-combining practice. *Teaching Exceptional Children, 39*(3), 6–11.

Saenz, L. M., Fuchs, L. S., & Fuchs, D. (2005). Peer-assisted learning strategies for English language learners with learning disabilities. *Exceptional Children, 71*, 231–247.

Salend, S., & Salend, S. J. (1985). Adapting teacher-made tests for mainstreamed students. *Journal of Learning Disabilities, 18*, 373–375.

Salend, S. J. (2005). Report card models that support communication and differentiation of instruction. *Teaching Exceptional Children, 37*(4), 28–34.

Schirmer, B. R. (1987). Boosting reading success. *Teaching Exceptional Children, 30*(1), 52–55.

Schlichter, C., & Brown, V. (1985). Application of the Renzulli Model for the education of the gifted and talented to other categories of special education. *Remedial and Special Education, 6,* 49–55.

Schoen, S. F., & Bullard, M. (2002). Action research during recess: A time for children with autism to play and learn. *Teaching Exceptional Children, 35*(1), 36–39.

Schubert, A. (1997). I want to talk like everyone. *Mental Retardation, 35,* 347–354.

Shaaban, K. (2006). An initial study of the effects of cooperative learning on reading comprehension, vocabulary acquisition, and motivation to read. *Reading Psychology, 27,* 377–403.

Shenkle, A. M. (1989). Orchestrating the words. *Learning, 17*(5), 40–41.

Siege, L. S. (1995). Issues in the definition and diagnosis of learning disabilities: A perspective on *Guckenberger v. Boston University. Journal of Learning Disabilities, 32*(4), 304–319.

Simmons, D. C., Fuchs, L. S., Fuchs, D., & Mathes, P. (1995). Effects of explicit teaching and peer tutoring on the reading achievement of learning disabled and low-performing students in regular classrooms. *Elementary School Journal, 95,* 387–408.

Simmons, D. C., Fuchs, L. S., Fuchs, D., Mathes, P., & Hodge, P. (1994). How inclusion built a community of learners. *Educational Leadership, 52,* 42–43.

Skau, L., & Cascella, P. W. (2006). Using assistive technology to foster speech and language skills at home and in preschool. *Teaching Exceptional Children, 38*(6), 12–17.

Slavin, R. E. (1996). Neverstreaming: Preventing learning disabilities. *Educational Leadership, 53*(5), 4–7.

Smaligo, M. A. (1998). Resources for helping blind music students. *Music Educators Journal, 85,* 23–26.

Smith, S. B., Baker, S., & Oudeans, M. K. (2001). Making a difference in the classroom with early literacy instruction. *Teaching Exceptional Children, 33*(6), 8–14.

Stauffer, S. L. (1999). Beginning assessment in elementary general music. *Music Educators Journal, 86,* 25–30.

Sutman, F. X., et al. (1993). *Teaching science effectively to limited English proficient students* (ERIC/CUE Digest #87). New York: ERIC Clearinghouse on Urban Education (ERIC Document Reproduction Service No. ED357113)

Swanson, P. (1998). Teaching effective comprehension strategies to students with learning and reading disabilities. *Intervention in School and Clinic, 33,* 209–218.

Taylor, H. E., & Larson, S. (1998). Teaching children with ADHD: What do elementary and middle school social studies teachers need to know? *Social Studies, 89,* 161–164.

Therrien, W. J., & Kubina, R. M. (2006). Developing reading fluency with repeated reading. *Intervention in School and Clinic, 41,* 156–160.

Thompson, A. (1996). Attention deficit hyperactivity disorder: A parent's perspective. *Phi Delta Kappan, 6,* 433–436.

Thompson, K. (1999). Internet resources in the general music classroom. *Music Educators Journal, 86,* 30–36.

Thompson, S. (1996). *Nonverbal learning disorders.* Retrieved November 11, 2008, from http://www.ldonline.org/article/6114

Thurlow, M. L., Ysseldyke, J. E., & Silverstein, B. (1995). Testing accommodations for students with disabilities. *Remedial and Special Education, 16,* 260–270.

Tindal, G., & Parker, R. (1989). Assessment of written expression for students in compensatory and special education programs. *The Journal of Special Education, 23,* 169–183.

Tomlinson, C. A. (2004). *The differentiated classroom: Responding to the needs of all learners.* Upper Saddle River, NJ: Prentice Hall.

Torgesen, H. K., & Murphey, H. A. (1979). Verbal vs. nonverbal and complex vs. simple responses in the paired-associate learning of poor readers. *Journal of General Psychology, 101,* 219–226.

Tripp, A., Rizzo, T. L., & Webbert, L. (2007). Inclusion in physical education: Changing the culture. *The Journal of Physical Education, Recreation, & Dance, 78*(2), 32–48.

Turnbull, A. P., Turnbull, R., & Wehmeyer, M. L. (2007). *Exceptional lives: Special education in today's schools* (5th ed.). Upper Saddle River, NJ: Pearson/Merrill Prentice Hall.

Uhry, J. K., & Shepard, M. J. (1997). Teaching phonological recoding to young children with phonological processing deficits: The effect on sight-vocabulary acquisition. *Learning Disability Quarterly, 20,* 104–125.

Vallecorsa, A. L., & deBettencourt, L. U. (1997). Using a mapping procedure to teach reading and writing skills to middle grade students with learning disabilities. *Education and Treatment of Children, 20*(2), 173–188.

Vaughn, S., Elbaum, B., Schumm, J., & Hughes, M. (1998). Social outcomes for students with and without learning disabilities. *Journal of Learning Disabilities, 31,* 428–436.

Vaughn, S., Hughes, M. T., Schumm, J. S., & Klingner, J. (1998). A collaborative effort to enhance reading and writing instruction in inclusion classrooms. *Learning Disabilities Quarterly, 21,* 57–74.

Vaughn, S., Linan-Thompson, S., Kouzekanani, K., Bryant, D. P., Dickson, S., & Blozis, S. A. (2003). Reading instruction grouping for students with reading difficulties. *Remedial and Special Education, 24,* 301–315.

Voltz, D., Dooley, E., & Jeffries, P. (1999). Preparing special educators for cultural diversity: How far have we come. *Teacher Education and Special Education, 22,* 66–77.

Wadlington, E., Jacob, S., & Bailey, S. (1996). Teaching students with dyslexia in the regular classroom. *Childhood Education, 73,* 5.

Walczyk, E. B. (1993). Music instruction and the hearing impaired. *Music Educators Journal, 80,* 42–44.

Walker, L. M. (1993). Academic learning in an integrated setting for hearing-impaired students: A description of an Australian unit's efforts to meet the challenge. *The Volta Review, 95,* 295–304.

Welsch, R. G. (2006). 20 ways to increase oral reading fluency. *Intervention in School and Clinic, 41,* 180–183.

Whitaker, S. D., Harvey, M., Hassell, L. J., Linder, T., & Tutterrow, D. (2006). The fish strategy: Moving from sight words to decoding. *Teaching Exceptional Children, 38*(5), 14–18.

Williams, J. P. (2005). At-risk second graders can improve their comprehension of compare/contrast text. *Teaching Exceptional Children, 37*(3), 58–61.

Williams, J. P., Hall, K. M., Lauer, K. D., & Lord, K. M. (2001). Helping elementary school children understand story themes. *Teaching Exceptional Children, 33*(6), 75–77.

Willis, S. (1996). Managing today's classroom: Finding alternatives to control and compliance. *Education Update* (Newsletter of the Association for Supervision and Curriculum Development), *38*(6), 1, 3–7.

Wilson, G. L. (2004). Using videotherapy to access curriculum and enhance growth. *Teaching Exceptional Children, 36*(6), 32–37.

Wilson, R. (1996). Teachers building self-esteem in students. *The Delta Kappa Gamma Bulletin, 62,* 43–48.

Wirtz, C. L., Gardner III, R., Weber, K., & Bullara, D. (1996). Using self-correction to improve the spelling performance of low-achieving third graders. *Remedial and Special Education, 17,* 48–58.

Wolery, M., Katzenmeyer, A. L., Snyder, E. D., & Werts, M. D. (1997). Training elementary teachers to embed instruction during classroom activities. *Education and Treatment of Children, 20*(1), 40–58.

Xin, Y. P., & Jittendra, A. K. (1999). The effects of instruction in solving mathematical word problems for students with special learning problems: A meta-analysis. *The Journal of Special Education, 32,* 207–225.

Yoo, S-Y. (1997). Children's literature for developing good readers and writers in kindergarten. *Education/Print Source Plus, 118,* 123–128.

Ysseldyke, J. E., & Algozzine, B. (1995). *Special education: A practical approach for teachers* (3rd ed.). Boston: Houghton Mifflin.

Zadnik, D. (1992). *Instructional supervision in special education: Integrating teacher effectiveness research into model supervisory practices.* Bloomington: Indiana University, School of Education and Council of Administrators of Special Education. (ERIC Document Reproduction Service No. ED358646)

Zentall, S. S., Smith, Y. N., Lee, Y. B., & Wieczorek, C. (1994). Mathematical outcomes of attention deficit hyperactivity disorder. *Journal of Learning Disabilities, 27,* 510–519.

Zhang, J. (2003). Effective instructional procedures for teaching individuals with severe disabilities in motor skills. *Perceptual & Motor Skills, 97,* 547–559.

Index

CORWIN

A SAGE Company

The Corwin logo—a raven striding across an open book—represents the union of courage and learning. Corwin is committed to improving education for all learners by publishing books and other professional development resources for those serving the field of PreK–12 education. By providing practical, hands-on materials, Corwin continues to carry out the promise of its motto: "Helping Educators Do Their Work Better."